THE POLLEN LOADS OF THE HONEYBEE

DOROTHY HODGES

THE POLLEN LOADS
OF THE HONEYBEE

A GUIDE TO THEIR IDENTIFICATION BY COLOUR AND FORM

CONTAINING A CHART OF POLLEN LOAD COLOURS
RECORDED IN THE SOUTH OF ENGLAND
THIRTY PLATES OF POLLEN GRAIN DRAWINGS
FOUR COLOUR PLATES
AND OTHER ILLUSTRATIONS BY THE AUTHOR

LONDON
INTERNATIONAL
BEE RESEARCH ASSOCIATION

Published by, and obtainable from:
International Bee Research Association,
Hill House, Gerrards Cross, Bucks SL9 0NR, UK.

Registered office at the offices of
The Zoological Society of London, Regent's Park, London NW1.

This facsimile reprint has been financed by two Members
of the International Bee Research Association.

First published 1952 set in Perpetua and printed by

Precision Press, Teddington, Middlesex, UK.

Limited publication of Pollen Grain drawings from book 1964.

Facsimile of full original edition, with addenda 1974

printed by Goddards & Cawley Ltd., Hull, N. Humberside, UK.

Second facsimile of full original edition, with addenda 1984

printed by G. Beard & Son Ltd., Brighton, UK.

British Library Cataloguing in Publication Data

Hodges, Dorothy
The pollen loads of the honeybee. – [1st ed. reprinted] with addenda
1. Honeybee   2. Pollen
I. Title

638'.13   SF523   ISBN 0 86098 140 1

CONTENTS

The 1984 facsimile reprint contains the following material not in the 1952 edition:

Drawings opposite page 21 and on page 33.

Methods of Melissopalynology, after chapter 10.

FOREWORD

ON A HOT SUMMER AFTERNOON in 1947 Mrs. Dorothy Hodges came for the first time to the Bee Department at Liebefeld, an unassuming Englishwoman who hardly ventured to mention her great interest, pollen loads and their colours. But she soon thawed, and from then on the discussion was always lively, the conversation being carried on in a mixture of English, French and German; and if words failed, drawings were a help. Carried away by the spontaneous enthusiasm of my visitor I gladly introduced her to the details of pollen microscopy and the methods of making pollen preparations. This accidental meeting was soon to become a friendship, and so I have had the pleasure from year to year of following the development of this book from its beginnings to its completion.

The happy conjunction of artistic talents and training, with a gift for observation and a great love of bees, has enabled Mrs. Hodges to produce a work which offers something new and valuable both to the bee scientist and to the practical beekeeper. Who has not stood in front of a hive in the spring, and watched bee after bee slipping into the entrance with its coloured pollen loads ? At once one asks oneself from what plants have the bees collected those yellow, white, orange or blood-red loads. Up to now no book has given a satisfactory answer to these questions, for words alone are inadequate to define colours. The chart of pollen colours, which Mrs. Hodges has produced with skill and great patience, therefore meets a long-felt need in the literature of bees. In this chart the scientist will be interested specially in the shades of colour which occur in pollen loads of the same botanical origin, according to the weather, the amount and condition of the pollen available, and what is mixed with it. A set of drawings of pollen grains is included which are of outstanding artistic merit, and which offer the further possibility of identifying the pollen forms which are most frequently collected by bees. For the beginner these drawings will do good service also as an introduction to the pollen analysis of honey.

It is true that we already possess today an abundant literature on pollen analysis and pollen microscopy, but most of it is not published in English. Moreover some of these books and works are out of print, or else they were published in scientific journals only accessible to specialists.   But wide circles of beekeepers in England and other countries are greatly interested in pollen research; and this book is aimed at satisfying this interest.   Because the main emphasis is laid on the colour chart and the pollen drawings, the book is largely independent of language barriers, and will be appreciated in many countries.   May it achieve the wide circulation and recognition which it deserves.

LIEBEFELD-BERN   ANNA MAURIZIO

January 1952

PREFACE

DURING THE WINTER of 1946 the idea occurred to me, as an artist and a beekeeper, of making a colour chart of pollen loads. The Research Committee of the British Bee-Keepers' Association having recently been formed, I reported my idea to them through Dr. S. Gooding, and received from Mr. E. B. Wedmore, who was then Chairman, instructions on suitable conditions for controlled colour recording. To Dr. Gooding I also owe my introduction to microscopy, as a result of which I started to make some small coloured drawings of dry pollen grains taken from the pollen loads. Dr. C. G. Butler suggested that a series of large-scale drawings of swollen pollen grains would be more useful, and he kindly offered the help of the Bee Department at Rothamsted Experimental Station. Mr. Simpson showed me the methods used there to prepare pollens for microscopical examination, and he subsequently identified some of the pollen loads taken from bees at the hive entrance.

In 1947 I visited the Liebefeld Institute in Switzerland, and there I found a friend and ally in Fraulein Dr. Anna Maurizio, who showed herself keenly interested in the work, especially the colour chart, and her encouragement, help, and advice then and since have been invaluable.

Major H. A. Dade of the Commonwealth Mycological Institute at Kew has advised me on several problems, and Dr. Gwenyth Wykes of Rothamsted assisted in my experiments with artificial pollen pellets. Riddles of plant nomenclature have been solved by Dr. F. N. Howes of the Royal Botanic Gardens at Kew, and both he and Dr. Melville have identified plant specimens. Dr. Eva Crane has been a friendly and stimulating critic, and through her the resources of the Bee Research Association and its library have been at my disposal.

All this scientific support has been given to me generously and unhesitatingly, and I wish to thank all these kind friends to whose guidance I owe so much.

ASHTEAD, SURREY   DOROTHY HODGES

February, 1952

1. INTRODUCTION

THERE CAN BE NO BEEKEEPER the world over, who has not at some time paused at the entrance to a hive and watched the procession of pollen-laden bees returning from the field, their pollen loads either sombre with brown or black, or glowing with bright colours, orange, yellow, red, or green. This fascinating sight can be seen at any time during the active season, and gives rise to constant speculation as to the source of the loads. The aim of this work is to determine whether it can be stated with accuracy that this bee for instance returns from the clover fields, that from the broad beans, or that from the ling.

To the commercial beekeeper, and to the man who hires out his colonies to a farmer for the pollination of specific crops, this subject can be of real importance. The honey farmer wants to know whether his bees are working the plants which he knows will produce the best honey, and the farmer needs to be assured that his crop is being pollinated and that the bees are not working, for instance, dandelions instead of fruit. The identification of pollen loads at the hive may give a fairly reliable indication whether or not these needs are being met.

Large quantities of pollen are carried in the form of pollen loads into every honeybee colony during a single season. Reliable estimates suggest that from 44 to 70 lb are required by an average colony (12)[1] Honey supplies the carbohydrates in the bee's diet, and pollen supplies the protein, vitamins, fats, and minerals. This pollen is eaten chiefly by the young nurse-bees, and from it they elaborate brood food, the so-called 'royal jelly,' a rich, nitrogenous, creamy substance produced by the pharyngeal glands in the head. This is fed to the queen, and also to the young larvae in the early days of their development. Adequate pollen stores are essential in the hive at all times, but it has been found that fresh pollen brought into a colony provides a direct stimulus to brood-rearing (54). As there is a delay of at least five weeks between the laying of eggs and the production of bees old enough to forage, this stimulus must be available some six weeks in advance of the flowering

(1) The numbers in brackets in the text correspond with the numbers in the Table of References at the end.

of the main nectar plants, in order to ensure sufficient flying bees to gather the honey harvest. In the south of England there is a wealth of early plants and trees to satisfy this need.

A knowledge of the flowering times of the important sources is essential, but as districts and seasons vary so much, no calendar can be generally applicable. The British bee plants selected for inclusion here have been arranged in their approximate flowering order in the south of England. Since many plants give similarly coloured pollen loads the possibility of confusion is reduced by reference to the flowering period.

For the benefit of those who do not already know the process by which the honeybee collects and packs her pollen loads a description is given of this intricate process, with a set of original illustrations.

The research worker engaged in pollen investigations, and employing pollen traps for collection of pollen loads, uses the colour of the pellets to sort them into groups before positive identification under the microscope. In some countries in Europe the analysis of pollen in honey has reached a high degree of accuracy. It has been found possible to determine the geographical origin of many samples of honey by the combination of the various pollen grains taken from the honey. This book has no pretensions as a guide to this specialist subject, but the drawings have been made from pollen grains prepared by the methods generally used by pollen analysts and are therefore comparable with preparations made from honey.

Modern selective weedkillers and insecticides are becoming an increasing danger to bees, and identification of pollen loads taken from dead bees at the hive can be of service in tracing the crop which has been sprayed. The use of these chemicals, by destroying many of the wild bees which were formerly responsible for much of the pollination of seed and fruit crops, is bringing into prominence the need to maintain honeybee colonies in good strength for this important function in agriculture. Only the beekeeper can overcome this deficiency of pollinating insects, for he is able to control his bees, and by co-operation with the farmer can either remove his stocks or shut in the bees during the danger period of spraying.

All the illustrations are the work of the author, and the paintings and drawings have been made direct from quick sketches of living bees, or from anæsthetized or dead bees.

The plant names used are those given in the British Ecological Society's Check-List of British Vascular Plants (14) so far as applicable;

and the pollen grain drawings are arranged in plant families in the order of Bentham and Hooker's *British Flora* (7) except for those grains which are over 50 microns in diameter. These will be found grouped together after the Liliaceae (Plates 25 to 30).

It is hoped that the chart of pollen load colours and the drawings of the individual pollen grains will be of value to some and of interest to many, and that this work will provide a stimulus to fresh investigations in pollen research.

2. THE POLLEN PACKING PROCESS

A WORKER BEE in a normal colony spends about three weeks performing duties in the hive before she becomes a forager. When she starts field work she may visit flowers which yield both pollen and nectar, or flowers which only yield pollen, such as the wind-pollinated trees. In the former case she will arrive at the flower with her honey sac empty and will gather sufficient nectar to moisten her load as she works. In the latter case she will set out with her honey sac partly filled with honey taken from the hive. This was stated by Parker (43), who tested bees working on wild rose (*Rosa rugosa*), which gives pollen only, and on white sweet clover (*Melilotus alba*), which provides both pollen and nectar. A recent paper by Beutler (10) suggests however that this is not always so. Bees working on plantain (*Plantago*) which yields pollen only, and lime (*Tilia*), in both cases had their honey sacs well provided with honey to mix with their pollen loads.

This honey or nectar is used by the bee to mix the dry pollen into a paste-like condition suitable for packing her pollen loads. The bumble bee makes her pollen loads in the same way, but many of the solitary bees such as *Andrena* collect and carry their pollen dry.

This mixing of the pollen with liquid, either honey or nectar, or possibly a mixture of both, makes the colour of the honeybee's *pollen load* quite different from the colour of the *pollen* alone as it is seen on the anther of the flower. This distinction must be emphasized and has been fully demonstrated by Reiter (46), and see experiments facing page 32.

Comparison of a dry load of ling pollen (*Calluna vulgaris*) carried by *Andrena fuscipes* Kirby, with the colour of a honeybee's load of ling pollen as recorded in the Colour Chart, clearly demonstrates the change that takes place with the added moisture. It is interesting to watch this *Andrena* working on ling side by side with the honeybee, whose loads are so conspicuously darker.

It is easy to observe bees at work on poppies (*Papaver*). This flower has no nectar and all bees working it are collecting pollen only. The bee scrambles among the anthers and gets dusted all over with the dry pollen grains; she then leaves the flower, and while she hovers nearby, a complicated quick-moving action can be

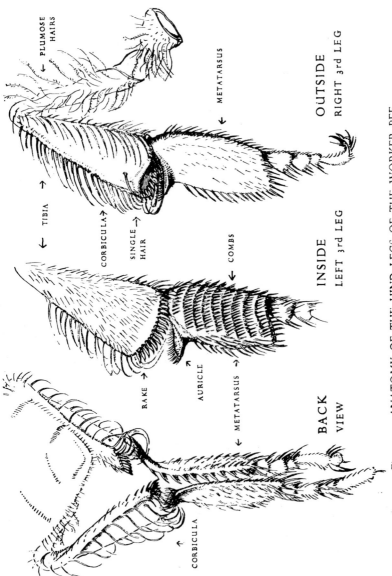

PLUMOSE HAIRS

METATARSUS

OUTSIDE
RIGHT 3rd LEG

TIBIA

CORBICULA

SINGLE HAIR

INSIDE
LEFT 3rd LEG

COMBS

RAKE

AURICLE

METATARSUS

BACK
VIEW

CORBICULA

Figure 1   ANATOMY OF THE HIND LEGS OF THE WORKER BEE
showing the position of the corbicula or pollen basket, the rake, the auricle, and the combs

observed, which has been described by Sladen (51), Casteel (13), and Beling (6). This can be summarized as follows.

The tongue is protruded and frequently stroked by the forelegs, which become sticky with honey which she has regurgitated (Fig. 4). The head and antennæ and front part of the thorax are then cleared of pollen grains by the antenna cleaners and the brushes of the forelegs. The back of the thorax is cleared by the middle legs and the pollen on the abdomen is swept off by the hind legs. This loose pollen becomes moistened with the regurgitated honey which the bee is continually conveying from her tongue with her brushes, and all this sticky pollen is transferred to the inner metatarsal brushes of the middle legs. Then the metatarsi of the hind legs are held together, and the metatarsi of the middle legs placed in turn

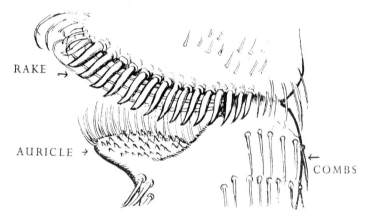

Figure 2   THE POLLEN PRESS
showing the rake, and the outward-pointing teeth and guiding hairs on the auricle
(inside of leg)

between them and drawn forward (Fig. 1). This leaves the pollen, now in a sticky mass, loaded into the rows of stiff combs on the inner side of the hind metatarsi.

When sufficient pollen is collected there, the final action takes place. At the distal end of the inner side of the tibia of the hindlegs is a strong rake (*rastellum*) composed of stiff pectens. This rake is held against the top of the opposite metatarsal combs and pushed downwards, thus raking out all the moist pollen in a compact mass into the pollen press between the rake and the auricle of the opposite leg (52) (Figs. 1 and 2). The joint between the tibia and the

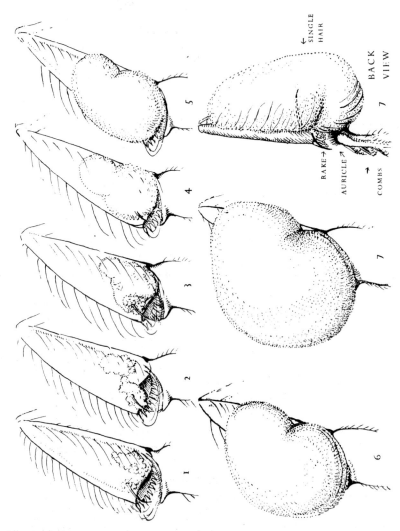

SINGLE HAIR

BACK VIEW

RAKE →

AURICLE →

COMBS ↑

5   4   3   2   1

7   7   6

Figure 3   THE PROGRESSIVE PACKING OF THE LOAD IN THE CORBICULA

tarsus is then closed and the paste-like pollen is squeezed in the pollen press and pushed outwards and upwards. Guided by minute teeth on the floor of the auricle and a fringe of hairs on the edge, it comes to rest on the smooth concave floor of the corbicula or pollen basket.

This action, repeated first on one side and then on the other, carries the pollen in small masses from the base of the corbicula upwards and forwards in a diagonal direction (Fig. 3). As the pollen pack gets larger the surrounding corbicular hairs hold the mass, some supporting the sides, and some underneath. The writer has observed that the single hair on the floor of the corbicula is gradually pushed upwards until it acts as a pin through the middle of the load where it is plumpest. This single hair, which may be found by cutting a load in half while on the leg, is so remarkable that it must be presumed to play an important role in the formation and security of the load. However, all attempts so far made by the writer to remove this hair under an anæsthetic have met with failure. It would be interesting to see whether a bee could success-fully pack a load if this hair were absent. During the packing operation the load is moulded, compressed, and perhaps lifted, by repeated pats with the tarsi of the middle legs, and thus the usual kidney-shaped load is formed.

Von Frisch (20) makes a delightful comment on the differences observed when bees were collecting pollen from dishes provided for his experiments: ' Individual differences in bees, which have been demonstrated in many experiments, are especially conspicuous when they are collecting pollen. Whereas one accumulates huge masses of pollen in a short time, another needs five times as long for the same amount, and a third shows but a very poor achievement after having worked as long as the other two together. In this they resemble human beings who also differ in their results—the one being quick and the other, though always busy, never accomplishes anything worth while.'

The whole process of pollen collection may be observed with greater ease if a jar containing willow (*Salix caprea*) is placed at eye level a short distance from the hive on a warm sunny day in early spring. The bees will usually find it quite soon and can be watched through a magnifying glass. They will often hang upside down by the claws of a front leg and use all five free legs to pack the pollen (Fig. 4).

A forager gathering mainly nectar may also pack pollen, but her loads are not so large as those of a pollen-gatherer. She is packing the pollen which her body hairs have unavoidably picked up as she brushed against the anthers to reach the nectar.   But she does not necessarily pack it; she may use her brushes to free herself of this pollen and drop it on the ground (5 and 12).   The writer has observed this pollen-discarding by hundreds of bees working a common lime (*Tilia vulgaris*) near the hives; during five years not a single bee has been seen to pack pollen from this tree, though some loads have been taken at the hive, possibly collected from another tree.   Lime pollen seems to be collected infrequently (44 and 53). On the other hand privet pollen (*Ligustrum vulgare*) is very often carried in large loads, but during a nectar flow from this plant bees heavily dusted with the pollen have been seen hovering and making the characteristic movements of pollen packing, but the corbiculæ

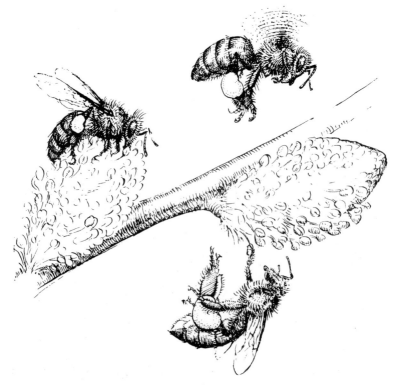

Figure 4   BEES WORKING WILLOW CATKINS (SALIX)

This shows one bee using her mandibles to scrape pollen from the anthers, another transferring honey from her tongue and loading her combs, and a third using her middle legs to shape the load

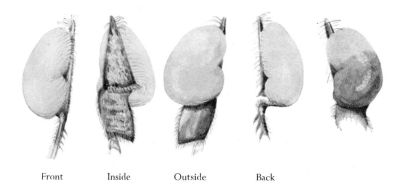

Front   Inside   Outside   Back

POLLEN LOAD OF MEADOWSWEET

(*Filipendula Ulmaria*)

MIXED LOAD
BERBERIS–
DANDELION

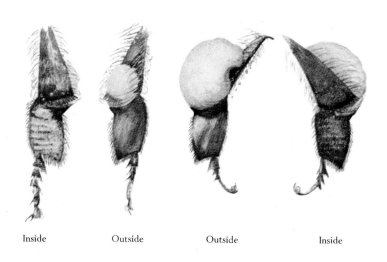

Inside   Outside   Outside   Inside

UNFINISHED LOAD
OF MUSTARD
(*Sinapis Alba*)

FINISHED LOAD
OF KNAPWEED
(*Centaurea Nigra*)

THE HONEYBEE CORBICULA, SHOWING THE "SPINDLE HAIR"

Drawing published by Dorothy Hodges in an article in *Bee World* 48(2) : 58-61 (1967)

remained empty, and the pollen fell loosely from the bottom row of the metatarsal combs. During this action it must be assumed that the joint between the tibia and the tarsus is kept closed, and indeed the position of the leg is quite different. If a hovering ' pollen packing ' bee is observed from the side, the frontal line of tibia and tarsus appears to be curved forwards, as contrasted with the slightly backward sweep of the line in a ' pollen discarding ' bee. In the latter no pollen grains can be observed loaded under the rake, and indeed the discarding bee seems to be using the row of metatarsal combs at the base of the tarsus to rake the opposite tarsus free from the dry pollen, which has had no honey or nectar added to it.

When a bee is collecting pollen from plants whose pollen is not abundant, the mandibles are used to bite and scrape the pollen off the anthers, and the pollen is packed while the bee rests on the flower, the back legs being thrust out beneath the raised abdomen.

Occasionally a bee will visit more than one flower species to gather pollen, and this results in a ' mixed ' pollen load. Betts (8) describes two kinds of mixed loads, the ' M ' type and the ' S ' type. In the ' M ' type the pollens from two or more species are mingled in the corbicula, which results in a uniform and possibly new colour. The ' S ' or segregated load is one in which the pollens are packed in blocks of different colours. One of the colour plates shows an ' S ' type load taken from a bee working dandelion (Taraxacum) which was growing at the foot of a berberis (Mahonia aquifolia). The position of the pollen collected first from the shrub is at the top of the corbicula.

When the load is complete—normally in from three to eighteen minutes (47)—the bee returns to her hive, usually quite free from loose pollen grains, all having been neatly packed in her corbiculae. But there are exceptions to this general rule. There seem to be times when she is unable to reach parts of her body, and if the structure of the plant she has visited is so arranged, she returns with specific parts of her body dusted. The disposition of this loose pollen has been noted by various writers (27, 31, 32, 35, 44), and considered in conjunction with the pollen-load colour can provide a valuable clue to the identity of the plant source.

If a bee has found a source offering sufficient pollen for fresh workers, she will on her return to the hive attract the attention of the other bees, and by giving off the scent of the flower and by her dance on the comb, will communicate the direction and distance of her find (20, 21).

3. PLANT SPECIES AND FLOWERING DATES

THE DATES and duration of flowering of plants vary from district to district, and from season to season, especially in the spring, and if pollen loads are to be correctly identified at the hive by their colour, constant observation of the flowers available is required. The district in which an apiary is situated, its soil conditions and climate, determine the flora available to the bees and govern their choice of forage. This phenological observation of flowering dates of important bee plants within reach of an apiary is part of the normal routine of every successful beekeeper. A paper on the subject was read at the XIV International Beekeeping Congress by Jeffree (29) with reference to his own observations in Aberdeenshire, in which methods of making recordings were suggested.

The weather and temperature play a large part also in deciding which flowers are visited each season. In some years the flowers succeed each other and the bees work each in turn, but in other years cold weather may delay flowering, and these retarded flowerings coincide with those which would otherwise follow them. This happened in the south of England in 1942, 1947 and 1951, when long cold spells in the spring delayed flowering; and when the weather broke, early and late spring flowers were out at the same time.

TABLE 1

YEAR	ORNAMENTAL Prunus cerasifera	PLUM P. domestica v. Early Rivers	APPLE Malus pumila v. Beauty of Bath	WHITE HORSE CHESTNUT Aesculus hippocastanum	LIME Tilia vulgaris
1941	Apr. 11	No record	May 17	No record	June 25
1942	Apr. 25	Apr. 25	May 1	May 24	June 30
1943	Feb. 24	Apr. 3	Apr. 15	May 8	June 11
1944	Mar. 15	Apr. 12	Apr. 27	May 11	June 24
1945	Mar. 9	Apr. 1	Apr. 12	Apr. 18	June 24
1946	Mar. 18	Apr. 3	Apr. 16	Apr. 30	July 1
1947	Apr. 15	Apr. 24	May 6	May 8	June 26
1948	Mar. 6	Mar. 23	Apr. 12	Apr. 22	June 17
1949	Feb. 17	Apr. 5	Apr. 16	Apr. 26	June 23
1950	Feb. 27	Mar. 26	Apr. 22	May 9	June 27
1951	Apr. 1	Apr. 20	May 9	May 16	July 1

Table I is a record made by the writer for eleven successive years at Ashtead in Surrey, of the dates on which single specimens of five species of trees growing near the apiary began to flower. The result shows that the difference recorded for ornamental prunus (*Prunus cerasifera*) has been as much as nine weeks, whereas the greatest difference recorded for lime (*Tilia*) is three weeks.

For these reasons, and because of the difficulty of assessing the beginning, ending, and peak of flowering, the compiling of a calendar of species which would be generally applicable has been found impossible. Nevertheless, an attempt has been made to arrange the species in the Colour Chart in the approximate order of their flowering sequence in the south of England.

The Chart includes those plants which are generally regarded as supplying most of the nectar obtained in the British Isles, most of them being important sources of pollen also. To this list has been added a selection of the many other useful plants which are sources of nectar and pollen. These contribute to the day-to-day food of the bees, and by their prevalence in some districts may be important. In the very early spring, when a fresh intake of pollen is vitally necessary, and when at the same time the bees are limited by temperature to short distance flights, every flower within reach of the hive becomes important, and in particular the flowering trees such as elm (*Ulmus*), poplar (*Populus*), and ash (*Fraxinus*). A few of these trees near the hive provide a vast foraging area (53). The alders (*Alnus*) and hazels (*Corylus*), though smaller, bear an abundance of catkins and are very favourite sources of pollen, especially in woods which provide valuable shelter from wind.

Garden flowers have been included where it has been thought they have sufficient interest. Even in January bees have been observed working laurustinus (*Viburnum tinus*) and *Erica carnea*, which flower nearly all the winter, but these and snowdrops (*Galanthus*) and *Crocus*, are only important in residential districts in case of scarcity of other sources near enough to the hives.

Observant beekeepers will sometimes find that some little-known plant is proving to be a useful source of forage. The list of species included here cannot of course be comprehensive, and for a fuller list of British bee plants the reader is referred to Howes' *Plants and Beekeeping* (27), and Harwood's *British Bee Plants* (24).

4. COLOURS OF POLLEN LOADS

THE COLOURS of pollen loads have been described in words by many writers, and these descriptions show that in some cases there is a considerable divergence of opinion.

It may be true, as some writers say, that the colour vision of individual observers differs, but this explanation has never satisfied the author. There are many factors to be considered which influence colour vision. It is difficult or even impossible to convey colour in words. For example, if several people with normal colour vision are viewing a colour specimen at the same time they may use different descriptive terms. But if the same people were viewing the same specimen, each under different conditions, they would be actually receiving different colour sensations.

The artist refers to colour under the terms: *Local Colour, Reflected Colour, Induced Colour.*

Suppose he is looking at a blue jug on a yellow cloth against a grey background. The *local* colour of the jug is blue, but some of the yellow cloth will be *reflected* in the surface of the jug. And the complementary colour of blue, which is orange, will be *induced* in the grey background, particularly near the outline of the jug.

Ostwald in his book *Colour Science* (41), speaking of his 'chromatic circle' (the colours of the spectrum arranged in a circle), describes this phenomenon under the heading 'Chromatic Contrast':—

'Here the hues of adjacent colour panels do not appear to be uniform. If for instance we observe the violet portion then every panel on the red side has a bluish edge and on the blue side a reddish edge, which is strongest on the boundary, and which exhibits a rapid but even gradation into the normal hue of the surface. Here the effect may be described by saying that two surfaces of different colours influence one another in such a way that each colour moves the other towards the opposite side of the chromatic circle, and that the closer the proximity of the colours the stronger is this effect.'

On the same subject and under the heading 'Induced colour', Jan Gordon says in his book *A Step-ladder to Painting* (22):—

'We have all at one time or another marvelled at the intense and lovely blue of the night as seen from within a lighted room. And who has not felt the disappointment when, on going out, the night has quickly greyed off to insignificance ? The intense blueness of the night was *induced* by the orange quality of the artificial lighting. Had the indoor lighting been crimson, the night would have seemed *green;* had the indoor lights been *yellow,* the night would have seemed *violet.* A positive colour always tends to change the colour near it to its complementary tint.'

The colours and their complementaries are as follows:— Green—Crimson; Orange—Blue; Blue-violet—Yellow.

It is possible that this aspect of colour vision may have influenced the colour descriptions given by different observers who, although perhaps describing the same colours, may have been viewing them against different backgrounds, for example against a brown hive, a white hive, or in the hand.

Colour may also be *reflected* in pollen loads from a blue sky or from yellow clouds. As an example, the blue-green loads of rosebay willowherb (*Chamaenerion angustifolium*) which appear exceptionally brilliant at the hive entrance, are far less so when taken to the studio for recording. This suggests that the blue of the sky was being reflected on to the glistening surface of the load, making it appear bluer (or this may be a case of induced colour due to the golden colour of the bee's body).

METHODS USED FOR COLOUR RECORDING

Having always been fascinated with this subject the author decided in 1946 to make a colour chart of pollen loads from the principal bee plants. The method adopted was to catch the bees as they worked on the various plants, choosing those with large enough loads to provide a satisfactory pellet. The bees were caught by the wings and held until the pellet had been scraped off the leg, either with the point of a pen-knife or more often with the finger-nail. If working near the house the bees were caught in cages (made from pipe-cover queen cages) and released against a window and caught by hand in the same manner. The loads were then recorded at once.

The conditions under which the recordings were made conformed to the recognized methods laid down for colour matching. The first requisite is a good north light, avoiding the evening hours when the light is likely to be yellow. Fortunately, days suitable for bees to work also provide the good light necessary for painting.

The pellets were laid on white paper and lightly patted to make a uniform flat surface. After a few experimental dabs to find the exact match, a surface about $2\frac{1}{2}$ by 1 inches was painted. Any colour which when dry (about ten minutes later) was not correct was discarded, and another recording made. This is an essential condition of water-colour painting as this medium tends to dry lighter, depending largely on the colours used. The colour strips were then cut into two pieces to provide duplicates.

Water-colour was chosen for the recording because this medium had been used for a long time by the author, and colour mixing needs experience to get exact results. Oil colours might have been used but the apparatus is not so easily portable as is desirable in this work. The following Winsor and Newton's Artist's water-colours, which have a high reputation for permanence, were used throughout:—

Aureolin	Venetian red	Prussian blue
Cadmium yellow	Light red	Cobalt
Yellow ochre	Burnt sienna	Permanent blue
Raw sienna	Alizarin crimson	Ivory black

A very large number of the loads were recorded with varying mixtures of Aureolin, Light red, and Ivory black.

During the first season single-colour recordings were made from as many species as possible, on the assumption that this was sufficient. But during the year two species, ling (*Calluna vulgaris*) and ivy (*Hedera helix*), recorded on two different occasions, gave such widely different results that it was decided to make several colour recordings from each plant species.

The first of these multiple recordings was made from a single specimen of ornamental prunus (*Prunus cerasifera*), two or three bees being taken from the tree every few hours for several days. The range of colour recorded was from dark brown to light tan, the lightest and brightest being recorded from midday onwards when the flowers were newly opening, and the bees were collecting the pollen as soon as it was released by the anthers. Early morning loads were nearly always dark in colour. These experiments have been fully described elsewhere (26).

Thus it became obvious that if recordings were made repeatedly from one individual plant, variations in colour occurred. Therefore, each species has had to be recorded over and over again until a range of colour could be established for each.

After five seasons' work nearly all the most important bee forage plants in southern England have been covered. This has demanded much patient work, first in seeking out the required plants growing in sufficient numbers to make an adequate foraging area, and secondly, near enough to an apiary to find bees working the blossoms. Even after these conditions were satisfied it was sometimes found that the bees were working the crop for nectar only, and little or no pollen was to be seen in their corbiculæ. This ' small-game hunting ' has proved to be a quite fascinating occupation, attended by all the thrills of any other sort of hunting—and the quarry has seldom lost her life.

In the case of high trees with the bees working out of reach, specimens of flowers were taken, and microscopical slides made of the pollen. Then loads were watched for at the hive entrance when these sources were known to be in flower near the hives. Many trees such as poplar (*Populus*), elm (*Ulmus*), oak (*Quercus*), and birch (*Betula*), being wind-pollinated, produce pollen profusely, which clings to the body-hairs of the visiting bee. When this tell-tale dusting was seen at the hive these bees were caught on the alighting board and their loads identified under the microscope.

As proficiency was gained in determining the origin of loads, more work could have been done at the hive entrance with the use of a pollen trap, but for the sake of accuracy this has been avoided. This decision was reached when it was found that many species belonging to the same family, such as Rosaceae, Salicaceae, Aceraceae, Cruciferae, etc., were very difficult to separate even by the colour of the pollen load and by microscopical examination of the grain. Therefore, the loads have only been taken at the hive when other methods of catching the bees on the trees have proved impossible.

COLOUR CHARTS AND COLOUR TERMINOLOGY

In the course of time we may hope to have an authoritative colour system, universally recognized and easily obtainable, by which colours can be named or numbered. At present there are two main colour systems based on scientific principles, the Ostwald and the Munsell. The Ridgeway system has been used extensively by scientists but seems likely to be superseded. H. A. Dade's monograph on *Colour terminology in biology* (15), seeks to establish a common vocabulary for the use of scientists. It needs to be used in conjunction with a recognized colour chart.

These systems of colour recording have been consulted by the author, but the steps between the colours are too great to permit the full colour range of pollen loads to be recorded in this way.   The *Dictionary of Color* by Maerz and Paul (30) has been found the most suitable, and all the colours with very few exceptions have been recorded by the letters and numbers in this publication.   Unfortunately, reference to it would not assist the ordinary reader, for only a few copies seem to be available in libraries in this country. It contains seven thousand colours which cover nearly the whole range of pollen loads except a few of the bright greenish-yellows, such as privet and charlock.

In the absence of a universal colour system it was decided to reproduce the colours and thus make them available to all bee-keepers.

A NECTAR-GATHERER AFTER A VISIT TO VEGETABLE MARROW (*Cucurbita Pepo*)

5. CAUSES OF THE COLOUR VARIATIONS

REASONS WHICH MIGHT ACCOUNT for the colour variations in pollen loads from the same species have been considered in the light of observations made when the colours were being recorded. It was found that dark loads might be expected in the early morning, after rain, after frost, or at the beginning and ending of the flowering period when few bees were collecting the crop; and that light loads might be expected in fine sunny weather when the flowers had just opened and when the available pollen was freshly released, and the bees were working the crop in large numbers (26).

CONDITION OF POLLEN

The pollens of different species are released or dehisced from the anther in different ways. Some dehisce slowly and gradually during the flowering period, blossom by blossom for several weeks. Others, including the wind-pollinated plants, give up their pollen in large quantities within a few days. Weather will influence this by hastening or retarding the blossoming, and will also affect the pollen already exposed on the anthers. Thus in dry warm weather the bees are able to work the blossoms when the pollen is newly released, and bring home pollen in its fresh state. But wet, cold weather keeps the bees at home, and pollen ready for collection on the anthers may change in colour, and may be collected in that state.

On this supposition the following tests were made. The results of these tests are recorded in detail opposite page 32, and the numbers of these colour squares are referred to in the text.

Tests with exposed pollen

The exposure of dry hand-collected pollen showed that some pollens lost their colour. Thus poplar (*Populus nigra*) faded considerably after four days in sunlight (squares 5 and 6), but hazel (*Corylus avellana*) tested under the same conditions did not (square 13). In another experiment willow pollen (*Salix caprea*) was laid on a glass slide which was kept in a closed box for six weeks. The colour changed gradually from golden yellow to pale yellow and then to pale green. Dry yew pollen (*Taxus baccata*) has a pale flesh tint when newly dehisced, but when shaken from the tree in the later stages of flowering it was found to be cream-coloured. Laurustinus pollen (*Viburnum tinus*) collected by hand after a night of frost in early spring was very dark.   On examination under the microscope it appeared greenish and translucent, while a sample of pollen from a freshly opened flower was opaque and white.   It seemed as if the pigment on the surface had disappeared, leaving the greenish contents visible through the exine, though the grains were not ruptured. Pollen taken from a newly opened blossom of *Prunus cerasifera* was more brightly coloured than that from a blossom which was ageing.

Effect of moisture on pollen grains

Pollen grains are in a shrunken condition after dehiscence.   If, for example, apple pollen grains (*Malus*) are taken from a mature anther and placed under the microscope they will appear to be a strong yellow in colour and shaped like a long grain of wheat.   If these grains are smeared with water they swell up and assume the shape of a triangular cushion, and the colour practically disappears owing to the expansion of the grain and consequent thinning of the pigment on the surface, rendering it transparent.

Adulteration

Adulteration of the pollen with dust or soot may take place near roads and in towns.   Examples of this can be seen in the darkest recordings of yew caused by dust, and of elm (*Ulmus procera*) caused by soot.   An artificial pellet was made from a sample of dry hazel

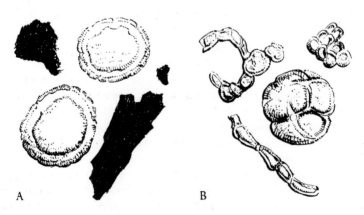

A   B

Figure 5   ADULTERATION OF POLLEN LOADS
(A) Soot particles in a load of elm (*Ulmus*)
(B) Moulds in a load of *Erica carnea*

pollen which had become dusty by exposure, and the result is seen at square 15. Another type of adulteration can be caused by moulds appearing in the loads. Dr. Maurizio sent the writer a series of loads of *Erica carnea* with and without these moulds, in which the change of colour to a dark greenish-brown was obvious. At Rothamsted (53) it was stated that many red clover (*Trifolium pratense*) loads were darkened by the inclusion of dark fungus spores.

EXPERIMENTS WITH ARTIFICIALLY MADE POLLEN PELLETS

By the courtesy of Dr. C. G. Butler, and with the help of Dr. Gwenyth Wykes, to whom I am greatly indebted, a series of experiments was carried out at the Bee Department of Rothamsted Experimental Station in 1951.

Nature of mixing material

The first experiment was designed to show the changes in colour observable when artificial pollen pellets were made with a variety of materials, using accurately weighed samples of dry hand-collected pollen, and sugar solutions. In the first series 9 mg. of dry pollen from both hazel (*Corylus avellana*) and poplar (*Populus nigra*) were mixed with 8 mg. of dark honey, light honey, and sugar syrup respectively—each a 38 per cent. sugar solution. The dry pollen and sugar solutions were weighed in a torsion balance and placed in watch glasses, mixed into pellets approximating in size to those collected by a bee, and recorded in colour.

The results obtained proved conclusively that the colour of the honey (or the lack of colour in sugar syrup) directly affected the colour of the pollen pellet. Thus the dark and light honey produced slight but definite differences in colour, and the sugar-syrup pellet was brighter than either (squares 1, 2, 3 and 7, 8, 9). In the case of hazel the range of colour in fact corresponded almost exactly with the range recorded for natural pollen loads. (No black poplar bee-collected loads were recorded, so that no comparisons could be made.)

These artificial pollen pellets were left in the laboratory overnight, and next day the colours were recorded again. An interesting difference was observed. The pellets of hazel pollen had changed colour considerably (squares 10, 11 and 12), though the difference between the samples remained; but the pellets of poplar had changed very little. This test demonstrates that in some cases pollen loads which are air-dried even for a short time are not comparable to fresh loads.

Dr. Wykes secured a sample of nectar (10 per cent sugar concentration) from the crown imperial (*Fritillaria imperialis*) which is unusual in that its nectar contains only glucose and fructose, and no sucrose (9, 59). An 8 mg. sample of this nectar was mixed with 9 mg. of poplar pollen. The resulting pellet appeared a paler and brighter yellow than the pellet made with the sugar syrup in a 38 per cent solution (square 4).

Amount of mixing material

The second experiment was designed to show whether the *amount* of sugar solution caused variation in the colour. Two weights of light honey, 8 mg. and 12 mg., were each mixed with 9 mg. of dry hazel pollen. The two pellets showed a marked difference in colour, the greater amount of moisture (square 14) producing a darker and greener pellet than the smaller amount (square 8).

(The first series of experiments gave results similar to those carried out by the writer in 1948 (26), when dry yew pollen was used, but as no accurate measurements were made at that time the results could not then be regarded as valid.)

CONCLUSION

The results of the foregoing experiments allow one to conclude that some of the colour variations are brought about by:—

(a) the condition of the pollen when gathered,

(b) the amount of the moisture used by the bee in making the load,

(c) the colour and nature of the moistening material used by the bee,

(d) the inclusion of adulterants such as dust, soot, or fungus spores, present on the flower at the time of collection.

These findings show that under all conditions there will be slight or considerable variation in the colour of pollen loads on bees working any plant species, or even a single specimen of that species. This may be due to the behaviour of the individual bee in the amount of mixing material used, and to the colour of that material, i.e., honey from the combs or nectar from the plant. Bees which are extending a foraging area, or lingering late on a deserted one, may collect pollen which has changed colour, or which has become contaminated. Moreover, weather conditions which may change the colour of the

ARTIFICIALLY MADE POLLEN PELLETS
EFFECT OF NATURE & AMOUNT OF MIXING MATERIALS

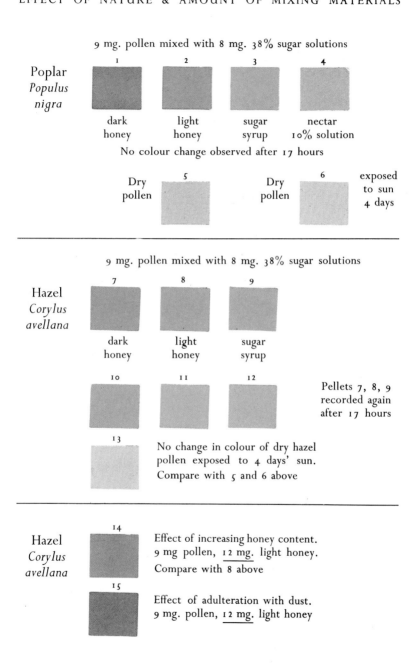

9 mg. pollen mixed with 8 mg. 38% sugar solutions

Poplar
Populus nigra

1   2   3   4

dark honey   light honey   sugar syrup   nectar 10% solution

No colour change observed after 17 hours

Dry pollen   5   Dry pollen   6   exposed to sun 4 days

9 mg. pollen mixed with 8 mg. 38% sugar solutions

Hazel
Corylus avellana

7   8   9

dark honey   light honey   sugar syrup

10   11   12

Pellets 7, 8, 9 recorded again after 17 hours

13

No change in colour of dry hazel pollen exposed to 4 days' sun. Compare with 5 and 6 above

Hazel
Corylus avellana

14

Effect of increasing honey content. 9 mg pollen, 12 mg. light honey. Compare with 8 above

15

Effect of adulteration with dust. 9 mg. pollen, 12 mg. light honey

pollen on the plant will produce a general effect on the colour of the pollen loads of all bees collecting at any one time.

When all the above-mentioned factors have been taken into account the possibility cannot be excluded that the colour of pollen grains on the anthers of individual specimens of a species may differ. Such differences have attracted particular attention in the green grains of purple loosestrife (*Lythrum salicaria*) on which much work has been done (49, 50).

PROGRESSIVE POLLEN PACKING SHOWN IN FOUR MIXED LOADS

These rare mixed pollen loads were found in Switzerland in a pollen trap. The bees had been working *Ranunculus* and *Geum* whose pollens differ in colour, one yellow and the other orange. The pattern reveals that the bee, when moulding the pollen in the later stages of packing, presses and lifts the load so that it rotates round the spindle hair in a spiral movement upwards.

The mark made by the spindle hair can be seen at the base of each load.

The single or "spindle" hair rises conspicuously from the highly polished floor of the corbicula. In an experiment it was shown that if the hair was cut off a bee had difficulty in packing and retaining a full load during its flight back to the hive. One such bee had a full load of 10.1 mg on one leg, and only 3.5 mg on the leg without the spindle hair.

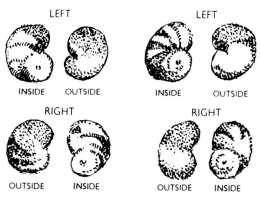

LEFT   LEFT

INSIDE   OUTSIDE   INSIDE   OUTSIDE

RIGHT   RIGHT

OUTSIDE   INSIDE   OUTSIDE   INSIDE

DOROTHY HODGES 1974

The drawings are similar to those published by Dorothy Hodges in an article in *Bee World*
35(2) : 31-32 (1954)

6. OTHER AIDS TO IDENTIFICATION

SHAPE AND SIZE OF LOADS

SOME ASSISTANCE is provided by the shape and size of the load, and the disposition of loose pollen on the body. Although not entirely reliable these evidences taken together can be very helpful indeed (31, 32, 35, 37, 44, 53). For example, white clover (*Trifolium repens*) is nearly always carried in the corbicula in a half-sized compact kidney-shaped load, but charlock (*Sinapis arvensis*) is carried in a large, almost square, load, reaching nearly to the top of the corbicula and low down over the tarsus; and the forehead has a patch of loose pollen. The reasons for these differences in shape are not clear. Identification based on them can only be of value in fine sunny weather when the bees have returned to the hive after uninterrupted pollen-collecting trips. R. O. B. Manley (32) observes that white clover is always carried in small pellets, and almost every bee carries a little of it so long as the plants are yielding nectar. He also quotes Dr. Miller as having observed that so long as his bees were carrying the little brown balls of white clover pollen, he knew that no heavy nectar flow was on; but when the bees were working the flowers but no pollen loads were seen, he could be sure that a heavy flow was in progress.

DISPOSITION OF LOOSE POLLEN ON THE BODY

Loose pollen is sometimes seen dusted on the bodies of the bees. Different flowers, because of structural differences, leave their pollen on special areas of the bee's body. Examples of this have been observed by various writers (35, 44, 31, 27). The colour of this dry pollen is usually different from the colour of the load in the corbicula owing to the moisture used to pack the load. A good example can be seen when the horse chestnut (*Aesculus*) is in bloom; many bees are covered with pollen which is bright orange to brick-red, although the pollen load may be a deep rich red. Indeed, the nectar-gatherers also are copiously dusted with pollen, of which they have not rid themselves, especially underneath the abdomen and wings.

The writer once saw loads of bright brick-red pollen from the white horse chestnut corresponding to the colour of the loose pollen which seemed to be almost dry in the corbicula; but this applied only to occasional loads and may be exceptional.

Most of the wind-pollinated trees have so much pollen available that the bees return to the hives with their bodies freely dusted with loose pollen. Poplar (*Populus*) and oak (*Quercus*) are examples of this. Bees returning from yew (*Taxus*) are smothered with what looks like face-powder. Observation revealed that when the bee alights on an unopened yew blossom a small explosion occurs and a puff of pollen is shot into the air. One bee was seen so smothered in pollen that she drifted downwards, alighting on a gate which was the first object she encountered, in order to free her head from the blinding pollen dust.

Table 2, page 37, gives a list of some flowers which cause body dusting, and of the parts of the body affected in each case, numbered as in Fig. 6, page 36. Where the pollen loads tend to be characteristic either in shape or size this is indicated in the right-hand column.

An especially interesting case is that of toadflax (*Linaria vulgaris*). The bees working this flower receive a ‘ plaster ’ of hard-packed pollen on the back of the thorax, as if the bee has been marked with yellow paint.

Maurizio (35) describes how samples of bees marked in this way, were sent to Liebefeld by beekeepers in various parts of Switzerland; and in all cases the pollen was that of *Linaria*. The writer has observed bees leaving the hive with the yellow plaster still intact. The narrow structure of the flower causes the bee's thorax to press the anthers against the side of the flower as she forces her way down to reach the nectar in the spur.

It may happen that bees marked with yellow from the toadflax may change over to another species, and therefore it would not always be safe to assume that bees so marked have received this pollen from the flowers on which they are found. Percival (44) saw bees still marked on the thorax with the orange dustings from broom (*Sarothamnus*), but carrying the typical loads of hawthorn (*Crataegus*); in this case the change-over was obvious.

Besides the species mentioned there are others which leave their mark on the visiting bee; and the pollen thus transferred from flower to flower may be responsible for effecting cross-pollination in the species concerned. By catching nectar-gatherers on the alighting board and removing some of the loose pollen, these grains can be used to identify the source of the forage. In some cases nectar-gathering bees return to the hive dusted all over with loose pollen which they have neither packed nor discarded.

Figure 6 DUSTINGS OF LOOSE POLLEN
The numbered areas refer to Table 2

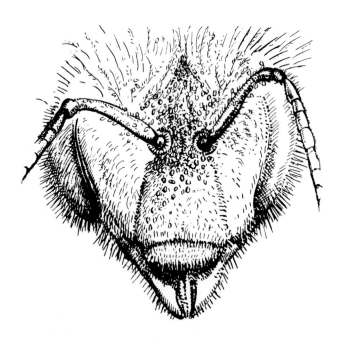

Figure 7 DETAIL OF POLLEN ON THE HEAD

TABLE 2

SPECIES	AREA OF DUSTING (N.G. = nectar-gatherers)	POLLEN LOAD
Anemone, *A. nemorosa*	I	Round and plump
Bluebell, *Scilla nonscripta*		Flat
Box, *Buxus sempervirens*	I, 3, 4	Very large
Brassica spp.	I	Very large
Broom, *Sarothamnus*	I, 5	Large
Buttercup, *Ranunculus bulbosus*	I (N.G. all over)	
Campanula sp.	I	
Chicory, *Cichorium intybus*	I	
Dandelion, *Taraxacum*	I, 3, 4	Large
Evening Primrose, *Oenothera biennis*		Large, untidy, trailing
Hazel, *Corylus*	I, 3, 4	Large
Hollyhock, *Althaea* sp.	N.G. I, 2, 3, 4, 5	No loads seen
Horse Chestnut, *Aesculus*	3, 4, 5 (and wings N.G.)	
Lupin, *L. polyphyllus*	3 and under wings	
Mallow, *Malva*	N.G. I, 2, 3, 4, 5	No loads seen
Maple, *Acer negundo*	I, 4	Large
Meadowsweet, *Filipendula*	3, 4	Large
Oak, *Quercus*	I, 3, 4	Large
Poplar spp., *Populus*	I, 3, 4	Large
Privet, *Ligustrum*	I, 3, 4	Large
Red Deadnettle, *Lamium purpureum*	I	
Ribes sanguineum		Flat
Rosemary, *Rosmarinus*	N.G. I, 2	No loads seen
Sage, *Salvia* sp.	2, 5	No loads seen
Scabious, *Knautia*	N.G. I, 3, 4, 5	
Thrift, *Armeria*	N.G. I, 2	No loads seen
Toadflax, *Linaria vulgaris*	3 plaster	
Traveller's Joy, *Clematis vitalba*	N.G. I, 3, 4, 5	
Vegetable Marrow, *Cucurbita*	I, 2, 3, 4	No loads seen
Willowherb, *Chamaenerion*		Flat
Yew, *Taxus*	I, 3, 4 smothered	Large

7. PREVIOUS WORK USING COLOUR IN POLLEN IDENTIFICATION

As PREVIOUSLY STATED, many beekeeping books give verbal descriptions of pollen load colours, but there are not many scientific papers dealing with this subject.

Dengg (16) in his comprehensive flower calendar for Austria, lists 2,400 bee plants and describes their pollen colours. The forty colour descriptions are arranged in a definite sequence, and give a colour picture which conveys understanding to the reader. Examples are:—creamy white, pale yellow, sulphur yellow, lemon yellow, golden yellow, wax yellow, dark yellow, muddy yellow, ochre yellow, egg-yolk yellow, orange, orange red, bright red, blood red, brick red, dark red, red brown, etc. These colour descriptions are given to all the plants listed. This appears to be the best alternative to actual colour matching to a colour chart.

Reiter (46) appears to be the first observer to use a colour dictionary for recording pollen-load colours. He worked by trapping bees on the plants concerned, and later matched the loads direct to the *Dictionary of Color* by Maerz and Paul (30) and to Webster's *New International Dictionary*. The chief aim of Reiter's paper is to demonstrate clearly the difference between pollen colour on the anther, and in the pollen load.

A few workers have used the colour of the pollen load as a partial basis for identification, either by direct observation at the hive, or in sorting the loads taken from pollen traps; their papers are shortly described here.

In an article in *Bee World* ' *The constancy of the pollen collecting bee* ' Betts (8) describes her work carried out at Camberley, Surrey, between 1908 and 1928 on observations made at the hive entrance. The pollen loads of the returning bees were removed with a damp paintbrush, and the source identified by microscopical examination. The colours were recorded in water-colour but were not published. A flowering calendar was compiled from the data thus obtained.

Percival (44) describes observations at a single hive in Wales from late April to late August 1945. Ten recording periods of thirty-five minutes each were spent each day at the hive, pollen loads being identified by colour as the bees entered, and counted by marking on a chequer board. Specimen loads only were identified by microscopical examination, and weekly maps were made showing the flora available to the bees within half-a-mile of the hive. A very detailed analysis is given of the species available and of their selection by the bees.

Jaxtheimer (28) working in Munich in 1946-47, captured samples of five successive pollen-laden bees at the hive entrances. Positive identification of all these loads was made by microscopical examination. The results are given in percentages for each plant species collected during each month, and comparison made with the results obtained by Synge and Percival. The colours of pollen loads are given, but no mention made of colour variation. An interesting point is the high proportion of lime (*Tilia*) recorded for June and July, though the total figures from which the counts were made were not very high. The highest percentage was 30.2 in July 1946 (*Tilia cordata* 28 per cent, *T. platyphyllus* 2.2 per cent).

At about the same time in 1945 and 1946 Synge at Rothamsted (53) and Maurizio at Liebefeld (37), both using pollen traps, were carrying out researches on the pollen intake of colonies; two side by side at Rothamsted, and two at different places in Switzerland, Liebefeld and Zürich. These papers make interesting reading and several important points emerge. Colonies differed in their selection from the pollens available even though in hives side by side. Different species are visited for pollen at different times of the day, and this is correlated with the times of dehiscence of the anthers of the various species. See also Percival (45).

Harris and Filmer (23) working in New Zealand, described differences in colour in pellets composed of the same pollen type in their paper *Pollen in Honey and Bee Loads*. Their suggestion that this difference in colour could be due to contamination by the colour of the pollen grains contained in the honey sac and then mixed with the load, could only be correct if very large numbers of pollen grains were present in the honey sac; this seems unlikely owing to the rapid disappearance of the grains from the honey sac (Maurizio 37).

Colour descriptions are given of the pollen loads analysed, but as these seem to have been sent a considerable distance after being collected in pollen traps, the colours would not be comparable with those of *fresh* pollen loads as recorded in the present work. But the descriptions of the amount of the variation found in some species are very interesting, especially those of thistle which are described as blackish, grey, lemon, fawn-white, and white. The two thistles, scotch thistle (*Cirsium lanceolatum*) and creeping thistle (*C. arvensis*) were the two species collected.   See Colour Chart No. 108.

Several other writers have recorded observations of variations of colour of pollen loads from a single species.   Reiter (46) records no less than twenty-two cases (15 per cent of the total) in which two colours were observed at the same time.   Betts (8) records one case, sweet chestnut (*Castanea sativa*), yellow but green in wet weather; Synge (53) records one, red clover (*Trifolium pratense*), due to adulteration by black fungus spores; Percival (44) records one, white clover (*Trifolium repens*), light to dark brown.   To these must be added Parker's observation (42), *Acer negundo,* green and yellow: and many variations in colour of pollen loads are mentioned in Harwood's *British Bee Plants* (24).

The percentages of mixed loads from two or more species of plants have been given as follows:—Betts (8) probably at most 3 per cent; Maurizio (37) 0.3 per cent; Percival (44) 0.1 per cent.

PACKING DANDELION POLLEN (*Taraxacum*)

8. DISCUSSION OF THE COLOUR CHART

THE RESULTS of colour recording during five seasons are presented in the form of a Colour Chart. The species are arranged in the approximate order of flowering observed in the south of England, so that it is possible to see close together the colours that may be expected at the hive entrance at any one time. Some species have been included because of the remarkable colour of their pollen loads, although not of great importance to the bee.

The colour squares have been mounted on a white background but it is suggested that a mask should be used over them. Masks can be made in various shades of brown or in black, according to the type of bee under observation or according to the colour of the background—hive or alighting board—against which the colours are to be viewed. This will also show the effect which colours have on each other as described in Chapter 4.

Each species is represented by three colour squares, referred to in the text as A, B, C. A is the colour of the darkest recording, B a medium recording, and C the lightest recording. These colours have been selected in many cases from five or six recordings, and therefore represent the extent of the colour range which has been observed, though they do not necessarily include the full extent of variation possible. The colour squares A in the left-hand column contain many recordings which can be termed exceptional, for they include those which were made under exceptional weather conditions, and those which were found to be adulterated. For example, elm A (*Ulmus*) was adulterated with soot; and yew A (*Taxus*) was adulterated with road dust. Bluebell A (*Scilla nonscripta*) was taken from a bee working late in the flowering period. Thistle A (*Cirsium arvense*) was taken from the first bee observed to work the crop at the start of flowering, and no other loads of this colour were seen again. Sweet chestnut A (*Castanea sativa*) was collected after a spell of rainy weather. *Prunus cerasifera* A was repeatedly recorded early in the morning, so also was apple A (*Malus pumila*).

The colour squares C are the brightest and lightest recordings made, when the weather was fine and sunny.

The aim of making the Chart has been to collect together the wonderful variety of colours carried by the bees into the hive, and to clarify, and perhaps reconcile, earlier differences in colour description. The result may have simplified the problem by replacing the vagueness of verbal description by actual reproduction of the colours, but it has also complicated the problem by demonstrating the variations which occur in pollen loads from the same species. Because of these variations confusion must inevitably arise when the colour range of one species crosses that of another. No two colour ranges are exact duplicates, but there are frequently one or more colour squares in a range which are identical with those of another species, and it is this fact which makes colour an unreliable guide to species whose colour ranges are similar and whose flowering periods coincide.

It would seem that the apparently conflicting descriptions of colour given by former observers were nearer the truth than was at first supposed, the conflict being due not to any error in observation or description, but to the assumption that there was one constant colour for the pollen load of any species.

One of the most difficult periods occurs in the spring when a large number of green pollen loads are being collected by the bees from different plant sources, the separation of which by colour alone becomes an impossibility. This ' green ' period occurs during March and April, and lasts until the flowering of the hawthorn (Crataegus). Later in the season green loads are not nearly so common, but in July there are the unmistakable brilliant green loads from meadow-sweet (Filipendula ulmaria), and in August the darker green of purple loosestrife (Lythrum salicaria). This latter species has a very remarkable peculiarity. Briefly stated, there are three types of plants, each of which is represented in a given population (56). The length of style varies, being either long, medium, or short, and is accompanied by stamens of two different lengths. The long stamens on the ' short style ' flowers have red filaments, and the anthers carry bottle-green pollen. The long stamens on the ' mid style ' flowers, also with red filaments, carry emerald-green pollen, while the short stamens have white filaments and the anthers carry yellow pollen. The ' long style ' flowers have medium and short stamens with white filaments, and both anthers carry yellow pollen. Not only is the colour different, but the three lengths of stamen bear pollen grains of different sizes. The green pollen grains are largest, being nearly twice the size of the yellow grains on the medium stamens, which again are larger than those on the short stamens. The bees collect all three sizes of pollen grains simultaneously, the resulting loads being various shades of green. These can be easily mistaken for ' mixed ' pollen loads until it is observed that all the grains have the same form. More rarely a bee collects a pure yellow pollen load from this species. This occurs when a bee confines her foraging area to a plant of the ' long style ' type. The writer records such a load in the Colour Chart, which was taken from a bee working a single isolated plant of this type. This load consisted almost entirely of the yellow pollen grains, but a very few of the larger green grains were also present, which must have come from another plant. Thus purple loosestrife provides the most striking example of variation in pollen-load colour. But this species is in a class apart, owing to the peculiarity of possessing pollen grains of two strong and distinct colours. Schoch Bodmer (49, 50) reports finding variations of colour and size in each of the three types of pollen grains of this species.

In the Rosaceae, an important family to the beekeeper, the genera are distinguished by differently coloured pollen. Pear (*Pyrus communis*) has a very distinctive grey-green load, whereas apple (*Malus pumila* or *Pyrus malus*), var. *Beauty of Bath,* has yellow loads in the lightest recordings and green in the dark. This tree flowers before any other variety of apple near the writer's apiary, and it is certain that these loads were not mixed with any other variety. With the ornamental crab apple (*Malus purpurea*) all the loads are green, a brighter colour than the green of pear. Maurizio (37) has found that different species of apple produce either green or yellow pollen loads, and the two varieties here recorded confirm this observation. Hawthorn (*Crataegus*) gives creamy-green loads, and this also applies to whitebeam (*Sorbus aria*) observed by the writer but not actually recorded. Rowan (*Sorbus aucuparia*) produces green loads. This group of the Rosaceae would seem therefore to be difficult to separate except by their flowering time.

The stone fruits (*Prunus* spp.) give loads of various shades from tan to brown; plum (*P. domestica*), cherry (*P. avium*), blackthorn (*P. spinosa*), almond (*P. amygdalus*), and the ornamental *P. cerasifera.* The pollen grains of the *Prunus* species have a characteristic striping or ' finger print ' marking on the surface of the grain, and it is this marking which makes possible the separation of the *Prunus* type from the *Pyrus* and *Malus* types. Blackberry (*Rubus fruticosus*) and raspberry (*R. idaeus*) both yield grey loads, the latter darker than the former.

The many species of willow (*Salix* spp.) whose flowering period covers many weeks, give a wide range of colour in their loads, from dark green to bright yellow.   Only one species *S. caprea* is recorded in the Colour Chart; but many others have been taken from bees at the hive, and the separation of these into their species has not been possible owing to the similarity of the forms of the grain.

It is very difficult to distinguish loads from the various members of the Cruciferae, many of which are very important to bees.   Both the colour of the loads and the form of the grains are so similar that they can be distinguished only by careful measurement under the microscope (40).   The species referred to include charlock (*Sinapis arvensis*), mustard (*Brassica alba*), white charlock (*Raphanus raphanistrum*) and all the *Brassica* family.

Two species which have given rise to very different descriptions of colour must be specially mentioned.   The loads of horse chestnut (*Aesculus*) have been described by some writers as crimson and by others as brick-red.   As now recorded in the Colour Chart the red horse chestnut (*A. carnea*) gives crimson loads, and the white horse chestnut (*A. hippocastanum*) brick-red loads.   The grains of these two species are illustrated on Plate 5, and it will be apparent that it is possible to distinguish the two species by the size, red horse chestnut being the larger.   Also illustrated are *Aesculus indica* and *A. californica,* the latter being the species which causes severe poisoning to bees in California (17).   Maurizio (36) describes the effects of poisoning in Switzerland by both white and red horse chestnut (*A. hippocastanum* and *A. pavia*), owing to the bees eating pollen, or nectar containing pollen, in too high a proportion.

In the case of bluebell (*Scilla non-scripta*) the loads have been described by some as blue, and by others as pale green.   Bees found working wild bluebells in a copse carried the pale green to yellow-white loads recorded in the Colour Chart, and bees working a group of cultivated bluebells in the garden carried the blue-green loads.   The pollen grains of these two varieties are identical.

One morning in May a large copper beech (*Fagus sylvatica* var. *purpurea*) was in flower within fifty yards of the apiary; for three hours the tree was alive with bees, and they carried large quantities of the copper-coloured loads into the hives.   After that time no more were seen, but only the pale-yellow loads from the common beech.

Several species (from different families) yield cream to white pollen loads in July and August which are difficult to separate by colour alone. These are the knapweeds (*Centaurea nigra* and *C. scabiosa*), chicory (*Cichorium intybus*), thistle (*Cirsium*), bindweeds (*Convolvulus arvense* and *Calystegia sepium*), *Veronica* spp. and borage (*Borago*).

The Colour Chart thus clearly demonstrates the difficulties of pollen identification by colour alone; nevertheless many of the important bee plants give distinctively coloured loads, so that, if these plants are known to be growing within the bee's foraging area, they may be identified fairly accurately at the hive (32, 44).

The species which can most easily be identified by colour include:—clovers (*Trifolium* spp.), broad bean (*Vicia faba*), sainfoin (*Onobrychis*), willowherb (*Chamaenerion*), ling (*Calluna*), horse chestnut (*Aesculus*), red deadnettle (*Lamium purpureum*), purple loosestrife green loads (*Lythrum*), blackberry and raspberry (*Rubus* spp.), meadowsweet (*Filipendula*), dandelion (*Taraxacum*) in early spring, poppies (*Papaver orientale* and *P. rhoeas*), scabious (*Knautia*), vipers bugloss (*Echium*).

During the flowering of some species the pollen intake cannot be considered as a guide to the species being worked for nectar. For example during the lime flow (*Tilia* spp.) although the bees may be working the flowers almost exclusively for nectar, few if any pollen loads can be observed, and these when seen may be small (53). This lack of pollen collection from species being worked for nectar has been found by the writer to apply also to snowberry (*Symphoricarpus alba*), flax (*Linum*), hollyhock (*Althaea rosea*), vegetable marrow (*Cucurbita pepo*), forget-me-not (*Myosotis* spp.), and bilberry (*Vaccinium myrtillus*). Statice (*Limonium* spp.) and thrift (*Armeria* spp.) are two other species not included in the Colour Chart owing to failure to find pollen loads, though bees worked the flowers for nectar. In parts of the country where they grow wild they may be important for pollen.

The identification of pollen loads by colour either at the hive entrance, or after collection in a pollen trap, can be *positively confirmed only by microscopical examination of the grains*.

9. LITERATURE AVAILABLE ON THE STUDY OF POLLEN GRAINS

THE THREE modern standard works in English on the study of pollen grains are by Wodehouse (58), Erdtman (18), and Faegri and Iversen (19). The first, which is mainly devoted to the study of those pollens which cause hay fever, gives a complete history of pollen morphology from the introduction of the microscope, which made this study possible, to the present day. Illustrations of many grains are given in the form of drawings, but the list of pollens does not include many of the bee plants.

Erdtman's and Faegri and Iversen's books deal with pollens found in peat and coal. Pollen grains have a very strong outer shell or exine which resists decay, and they can be found preserved in the layers of peat. By taking borings, and sifting out these pollen shells, the vegetation can be reconstructed as far back as the Eocene Age, six million years ago. For comparing living pollens with these pollen shells, the fresh pollen must be treated with chemicals to remove the contents. For this reason the illustrations are not comparable with slides made from fresh pollens.

There are two books in English on pollen in relation to beekeeping, one by Yate Allen (1) and another by Hayes (25), but both are out of print and can only be obtained from libraries.

For those who read German, Zander's books (60) represent the standard work on pollen in honey, containing comprehensive lists of all bee plants and fully illustrated with photographs. Another work on the same subject is Armbruster's (2, 3) with drawings by Oenike and Jacobs. These works are on sale in Germany, except for Zander's Vol. I which was destroyed during the war.

Dr. Maurizio is at present engaged on an important book dealing with her researches over many years on pollen, honey and bees, at the Bee Department at Liebefeld-Bern, Switzerland. Her extensive work on these subjects is to be found in articles and supplements to the *Schweizerische Bienenzeitung*. Her review in *Bee World* (39) gives the English reader a clear account of the methods used by pollen analysts to remove the pollen grains from honey, how to prepare them for examination, and how to count and assess their proportions. By these means it is possible, in some cases, to determine the geographical origin of honey.

10. PREPARING POLLEN GRAINS FOR MICROSCOPICAL EXAMINATION

POLLEN GRAINS, which carry the male reproductive cells of plants, appear to our unaided eyes as coloured dust, but under the microscope they are seen to be beautifully fashioned in a variety of shapes and sizes, and decorated with sculptured designs, according to the plant family to which they belong. High magnification is necessary to see these grains in their full detail, for they are very small. Pollens dealt with in this book range from six microns (forget-me-not, *Myosotis*) to 140 microns (hollyhock, *Althaea rosea*); one micron equals 1-1000th of a millimetre or 1-25,400th of an inch. These two grains can be seen drawn to the same scale on Plate 25.

The student of pollen in relation to beekeeping should build up a collection of microscope slides of pollens taken from the important bee plants and prepared in a way generally used by bee research institutes. These slides will serve as a standard for comparison with slides made from pollen loads or from pollen taken from honey. The drawings are intended to be used in conjunction with, and not as an alternative to, a collection of pollen preparations made with grains in a swollen condition and mounted in glycerine jelly.

Unprepared grains as taken from flowers or from the bee's pollen loads are in a dry and shrunken condition, the furrows and pores having in some cases disappeared inside the shell or exine. In this state the grains are difficult to identify, and it is usual to prepare them for examination by swelling them. Zander (60) describes the forms of pollens in both the dry and swollen states, and suggests that in order to learn the structure of the grains both conditions should be studied. It should be mentioned that the grain in its dry state is far stronger in colour than the swollen grain. One reason for this is that the swelling process thins the pigment on the surface (like a coloured balloon being blown up); another reason is that grains which have an oil-soluble pigment are left nearly colourless when the oil is washed off by the ether or alcohol, as for example, with red deadnettle (*Lamium purpureum*). Other grains retain their colour, such as charlock (*Sinapis arvensis*) and privet (*Ligustrum vulgare*), and appear as pale yellow. The colours of grains under the microscope of course, whether swollen or not, do not necessarily resemble the colours of pollen loads.

At the time of writing the Commission for Bee Botany of the International Union of Biological Sciences is studying the means to standardize methods for the preparations of pollens for pollen analysis in bee research.   Of the methods at present in use two are mentioned here.   The method given by Maurizio (39) in her review in *Bee World* ' *Pollen Analysis of Honey* ' is as follows:—

' Fresh pollen or whole anthers are put on a slide and moistened with one or two drops of ether.   Whole anthers are lightly pressed with a probe so that the pollen falls out.   Before taking the pollen it is desirable to keep the flowers in water indoors for a few hours so that the ripe anthers burst and release the pollen.   When the ether has evaporated the coarser parts are removed from the slide, and the pollen adhering to the glass is mixed with a drop of a solution of honey,[1] sugar or glycerine,[2] and the drop spread out on the slide and allowed to dry in the oven.   The slide is then closed with a drop of melted glycerine jelly.[3]   The swelling of the pollen in a solution of honey, sugar, or diluted glycerine, has the advantage that in a short time the pollen grains acquire the shape and size of those in the honey sediment.'

The usual method of extracting pollen from a honey which is to be analysed is by the use of a centrifuge.

' Ten grams of thoroughly stirred honey are dissolved in a reagent flask in 20 cc. distilled water; the solution is centrifuged (5 min. at 2,500 to 3,000 r.p.m.) and the liquid poured off the sediment except for the last few drops.   The sediment is stirred with a sterilized platinum rod, transferred to a slide, spread out a little, and dried in an oven at 30° to 37° C.   The dried sediment is now mounted permanently with a drop of glycerine jelly melted in a water bath.'

A simple centrifuge can be constructed at home if a fractional

---

(1) *Honey solution.*   Dissolve one part honey in two parts distilled water, boil for 15 min., add carbolic acid crystals (0.5 g. per 100 cc. solution), then filter several times through a fine filter.

(2) *Glycerine solution.*   One part glycerine to two parts distilled water.

(3) *Glycerine jelly.*   7 g. gelatine are shredded and soaked in 42 cc. distilled water for two hours.   Then 50 cc. glycerine and 0.5 g. carbolic acid crystals are added, and the mixture warmed and stirred in the water bath for 15 min., and filtered while hot through moistened glass wool.   If the jelly is to be stained, a few drops of a saturated alcohol solution of methyl green or iodine green are added before filtering, or a 10 per cent solution in water of basic fuchsin.

PACKING WILLOW POLLEN (*Salix*)

H.P. motor is available, the motor being mounted with its spindle vertical, and a cross-bar fitted to the spindle to carry at its ends the two metal containers for the glass flasks. Both containers and conical-ended centrifuge flasks can be obtained for a few shillings from suppliers of laboratory equipment. Some form of starting resistance is desirable, and precautions must be taken against accidents. If a centrifuge cannot be used the pollen must be extracted by precipitation as described by Yate Allen (1). Half an ounce of the honey is stirred into one ounce of water, and allowed to stand for 24 hours in a half-inch glass tube 20 inches long. This tube is open at the lower end, to which is attached by a rubber collar a small cup, preferably with a conical end from which the pollen can be easily removed after the liquid has been poured off.

The method used for the preparation of the pollens from which the drawings were made is that of Wodehouse (58), and is as follows:—

' A small amount of pollen . . . . is placed on the centre of a microscope slide, and a drop of alcohol added and allowed partly to evaporate. A second and third or even fourth drop may be added if necessary. The alcohol spreads out as it evaporates and leaves the oily and resinous substances of the pollen deposited in a ring around the specimen. The oily ring is wiped off with cotton moistened with alcohol, and, before the specimen has had time to dry completely, a small drop of hot, melted methyl-green glycerine jelly is added, and the pollen stirred in with a needle and evenly distributed. During the process the jelly is kept hot by passing the slide over a small flame, heating it just enough to sting but not burn the knuckle, which may be used to test its temperature. A number O cover glass, which has been passed several times through the flame while held vertically with the forceps, is then placed over the specimen, and the slide gently heated. If the amount of jelly has been judged correctly, the cover will settle into position, with the gelatine reaching its periphery just when the pressure of the cover begins to be taken up by the pollen grains. This amount must be learned by experience and accurately gauged, because a smaller amount leaves the grains crushed or flattened by the cover, or the mount incompletely filled, and a larger amount causes the preparation to be too thick for use with oil-immersion lenses.' *

In place of methyl-green the stain used was basic fuchsin which has the advantage of being permanent. Excessive staining of the

* By permission from *Pollen Grains*, by R. P. Wodehouse.   Copyright 1935 McGraw-Hill Book Company, Inc.

grains may obscure the detail, and must be avoided.   At the same time a second preparation was made of the grains in their natural colour, in plain glycerine jelly.

The beginner may be bewildered by the many positions in which the grains lie in a pollen preparation, but a full comprehension of the grains can only be gained if all these positions are studied. Only one, or in some cases two, positions of each species are illustrated, but it should be possible to find in a pollen preparation some grains which are lying in the same position as those drawn. Difficulty may also be found at first in seeing the fine details of the exine; the individual grains chosen for drawing have been those which by their position near the cover-glass have been seen in full clarity of detail, but all the grains in a preparation may not be so conspicuously marked.

The magnification necessary for pollen analysis is from 350 to 450 diameters.   For the examination of surface texture the use of an oil-immersion lens is recommended.   Two scales have been used for the drawings owing to the great difference in size between the largest and smallest grains; the drawings of the grains under 50 microns are magnified 1,500 diameters, and those over 50 microns 600 diameters.   No detailed measurements of the pollen grains are given in this book.   Each drawing can be measured by the scale given on each plate, but there are of course variations in size in most species.   Each grain selected for drawing has been chosen for its characteristic form rather than for its size.

Difference in size can be due to nutrition (50), and variety. Thus *Erica carnea* (Plate 19) is taken from a cultivated variety ' *Winter Beauty* ', and the grains in this preparation seemed to be larger than those taken from a wild variety growing in Switzerland. Apart from such variations there are some interesting species which have specific plant forms yielding different sizes of grains, such as purple loosestrife (*Lythrum salicaria* Plate 13) and buckwheat (*Fagopyrum esculentum* Plate 21) (27).   In the latter species the small form only has been illustrated, the larger form measuring up to 47 by 43 microns.   The Plumbaginaceae also should be noted, of which thrift (*Armeria* Plate 30) and sea lavender (*Limonium* Plate 30) are illustrated.   These plants yield different types as well as different sizes of grains on individual plants (4, 49, 50).

The grains of the Onagraceae, the willowherb family, Plates 26 and 27, are distinctive in the possession of strands of viscin which grow from them, and entwine themselves among the pollen loads.

Especially is this true of the evening primrose (*Oenothera biennis*), and it is these strands which cause the loads to be so unmanageable by the bees. The grains of the hairy willowherb (*Epilobium hirsutum*) are frequently found still joined together in groups of four. *Clarkia elegans* grains are a beautiful shade of pink under the microscope.

Correct identification of pollen grains is in some cases very difficult, and it is often possible to determine only the genus, or even only the family. A knowledge of the forms and sizes of the grains is essential, and every detail must be studied in comparison with the standard pollen slides. The detailed drawings of pollen grains will, it is hoped, encourage others to take up the study of this interesting aspect of beekeeping and botany.

Reprinted with permission from Bee World *51(3): 125-138 (1970)*

METHODS OF MELISSOPALYNOLOGY

by INTERNATIONAL COMMISSION FOR BEE BOTANY OF I.U.B.S.

(prepared by J. Louveaux, Anna Maurizio and G. Vorwohl)

In 1962 a second edition of "Methods of pollen analysis of honey" was issued by the International Commission for Bee Botany (I.U.B.S.). This was a revision of the first (1952) edition, and was needed because of the large amount of work on microscopical analysis of honey which had been done since Zander's basic studies in the 1930s.

The present—much enlarged—edition is the outcome of a meeting on melissopalynology (pollen analysis of honey) held at Hohenheim in 1967*. The layout follows the "Standard layout of a standard method of food analysis submitted to the Codex Committee on Methods of analysis and sampling *of the Joint FAO/WHO Food Standards Program (Codex Analys 68/8 June 1968)".*

1. SCOPE OF MICROSCOPICAL ANALYSIS

Microscopical analysis provides information:

1.1 about the geographical origin of honey,

1.2 about the botanical origin of honey.

Microscopical analysis allows additional statements:

1.3 about any contamination of honey with brood, dust, soot, etc.; about the yeast content (fermentation); about other microscopic particles not usually present in honey.

2. FIELD OF APPLICATION

2.1 The geographical origin can in theory be determined of any honey whose pollen had not been completely removed by filtering.

2.2 Determination of botanical origin is possible provided that the honey was extracted centrifugally. The pollen spectra of pressed honey or heather (*Calluna*) honey extracted by means of a "loosening" device, and of honey which has been filtered through diatomaceous earth or a similar material, are changed by the admixture or removal of pollen. The conditions necessary for a correct determination of the botanical origin of such honeys are no longer present.

In some cases it may be necessary to measure the amount of sediment and to determine the absolute number of plant constituents in order to establish whether the honey in question really has been extracted centrifugally (see 4).

3. QUALITATIVE MICROSCOPICAL ANALYSIS

3.1 Principle

Concentration of the microscopic elements by centrifuging the honey dissolved

---

* See Vorwohl (1968*b*)

in water. Examination and evaluation under the microscope of the sediment mounted with glycerine jelly.

3.2 Reagents

Kaiser's glycerine gelatine.

3.3 Apparatus

Laboratory centrifuge 2500–3000 rpm, relative centrifugal acceleration about 1350 g; centrifuge tubes with conical ends about 100, 50 and 10 ml capacity; microscope, magnification 320–450 × and 800–1000 ×.

3.4 Samples

3.4.1 The so-called laboratory sample should consist of 100–200 g honey.
3.4.2 By thorough stirring, the laboratory sample is transformed into the so-called test sample. If the honey is firmly crystallized, the sample should be softened by slight warming.

Dirty honeys are liquefied at 40°C and strained through cheese-cloth or through a fine sieve.

Comb honeys are carefully uncapped. The combs are held against a strong source of light in order to find out cells which contain pollen. By means of a pipette connected to a pump, the honey is then drawn out of those cells which do not contain pollen.

3.5 Procedure

3.5.1 Preparation of slides

10·0 g of honey are weighed and dissolved in 20 ml of hot water (not above 40°C). The solution is centrifuged for 10 min and the supernatant liquid decanted or drawn off. For the better removal of the honey sugars it is recommended that the sediment is dispersed again with about 10 ml of distilled water. The solution is poured into a small tube and centrifuged for 5 min. The entire sediment is put on a slide (as completely as possible) and spread out over an area about 20 × 20 mm by means of a thin glass or platinum rod. After drying, preferably by slight heating (not above 40°C), the sediment is mounted with glycerine gelatine, liquefied by heating in a water-bath at 40°C. The sediment can also be mounted with stained glycerine gelatine (see 5.2).

The use of Pasteur-pipettes is also recommended for transferring the sediment from the centrifuge tube to the slide, the capillary end having been closed by melting. The pipette may be used to disperse the sediment; the point is then cut off, and the dispersed sediment drawn off and blown out on to the slide.

The pipette should be handled with care in order to prevent the point splintering. The sediment constituents which remain in the tube are stirred up with a drop of water and pipetted a second time. The pipette is then rejected. This method allows an almost quantitative transfer of the sediment. As the pipette is used only once, no contamination (especially of pollens from other honeys) can be introduced during the transfer of the sediment.

Generally 10 g of honey are used for the preparation. If the honey is poor in pollen, the amount of honey may be doubled (Vergeron, 1964). If the honey is rich in sediment the residuum should be spread under two cover-glasses.

The microscopical examination of honeys rich in colloidal matter is facilitated if the honey is dissolved with diluted sulphuric acid instead of water (5 g concentrated sulphuric acid (H_2SO_4) added to 1 litre water. The colloids are dissolved for the most part by the acid and remain in the supernatant fluid during the centrifugation. By washing the sediment twice with water the remaining acid is eliminated. Otherwise the sediment is handled as described above. Another method for eliminating colloidal matter and small insoluble particles which render the examination of the pollen difficult is the filtration of the sediment dispersion through a millipore filter with pores from 3 to 5 μ. The pollen grains remain on the filter. They are washed out, centrifuged, and mounted as described above. Details of the filtration technique are given under 4.2.5.

3.5.2 Performance of microscopical examination

The determination of geographical and botanical origins is based on the identification and counting of pollen grains and other particles present in honey. This identification is made by reference to the literature and comparative preparations (see 5).

3.5.2.1 The analysis may be either orienting or complete. In the first case the analysis is limited to the identification of the most frequently occurring particles and to a search for certain significant characteristic elements in the sediment.

3.5.2.2 The complete analysis involves the identification of all pollen grains and other microscopic constituents in the sediment, so far as is possible at the present state of knowledge. With regard to counting of microscopic elements in the sediment, three degrees of accuracy are distinguished:

3.5.2.3 *Estimate:* This is conveniently done by counting 100 pollen grains and the honeydew elements corresponding to 100 grains.

3.5.2.4 *Determination of frequency classes:* This is based on counting 200–300 pollen grains and the corresponding honeydew elements. If the pollen spectrum contains few species, it is sufficient to count 200 grains, but if the spectrum is rich in species, 300 grains must be counted.

3.5.2.5 *Counts expressed in percentages:* Presentation of frequencies as percentages is permitted only if 1200 pollen grains are counted. The counts should be made on two slides (prepared independently) from the same honey.

3.5.2.6 In honeydew honeys poor in pollen grains, it is sufficient to count 50, 100–150 or 600 grains, according to the degree of accuracy required.

3.5.2.7 Pollens of wind-pollinated and of nectarless plants are noted separately. Important wind-pollinated plants in this context are: Gramineae (wild grasses, cereals, maize), Cyperaceae (sedges), *Rumex* spp. (sorrel), *Cannabis* (hemp), *Quercus* (oaks). Pollens of conifers (*Abies, Pinus, Picea, Juniperus, Larix, Taxus*), *Betula* spp. (birch), *Fagus* spp. (beech), *Carpinus* spp. (hornbeam), *Populus* spp. (poplar), *Alnus* spp. (alder), and *Corylus* spp. (hazel), are not important in honeys, nor are pollens of *Urtica* spp. (nettles), *Typha* spp. (reedmace) or Juncaceae (rushes).

The following plants are known to be nectarless but more or less entomophilous: *Papaver* spp. (poppies), *Plantago* spp. (plaintains), *Thalictrum* spp. (meadow-rues), Chenopodiaceae (goosefoot family), *Ambrosia* spp. (ragweeds), *Artemisia* spp. (wormwoods). Doubtful are the Cistaceae and *Filipendula* spp., which in general produce little or no nectar.

3.5.2.8 Abortive and mis-shapen pollen grains are counted, so far as they can be identified.

3.5.2.9 Honeydew elements consist of fungus spores and hyphae (especially those of sooty moulds), algae, and wax elements of honeydew-producing insects. A multicellular hypha, or a complex of spores, is counted as one element.

3.5.2.9.1 Plant-pathogenic fungus elements—e.g. spores of Uredinaceae (rusts), Ustilaginaceae (smuts), and Peronosporaceae—are noted separately from honeydew elements if they are present in appreciable quantities (Maurizio, 1959). Sometimes they are collected by bees with nectar, or occasionally bees make them into pellets like pollen. Finally, plant-pathogenic spores may contaminate honeydew as a sediment from the air.

3.5.2.9.2 The finely granulated and microcrystalline matter often indicates honeydew, but it is also found in some flower honeys and should be noted under "other constituents of the sediment".

3.6 Expression of results

3.6.1 The identification of pollen grains often cannot be performed as far as the genus or species. The use of scientific species and generic names should be limited to those which can be reliably determined.

If this condition is not complied with, a suitable note should be added after the scientific name in order to indicate that the term is used in a wider meaning, e.g. *Trifolium repens* s.l. (*sensu lato*), or *Trifolium repens* group (i.e. pollens which are identical with or very similar to *T. repens* in shape and morphological characteristics, but which may belong to another species, e.g. *T. resupinatum*, *T. arvense*). If detailed knowledge is not available, or if lack of time does not allow a closer identification, the pollen may be associated in larger groups (forms or types), e.g. *Teucrium*-form (a 3-colpate Labiatae pollen grain with opercula), or *Symphytum*-type (stephano-colporate Boraginaceae pollen grain); see Maurizio & Louveaux, 1967; Vorwohl, 1968a.

3.6.2 Presentation of frequencies

3.6.2.1 If the frequency of pollen grains is estimated, the following terms are used:
"very frequent" for pollen grains which constitute more than 45% of the total;
"frequent" for grains which constitute 16–45% of the total;
"rare" for grains which constitute 3–15% of the total;
"sporadic" for grains which constitute less than 3%.

3.6.2.2 If the frequency classes are determined, the following terms are used:
"predominant pollen" constituting more than 45% of the pollen grains counted;
"secondary pollen" (16–45%);
"important minor pollen" (3–15%);
"minor pollen" (less than 3%).

5

3.6.2.3 If at least 1200 pollen grains are counted, the frequencies can be expressed in percentages with an accuracy of $\pm 1\%$. The use of any digits after the decimal point is consequently not justified. Pollens whose frequency is 1 % or less should be quoted merely as "present".

3.6.2.4 If the frequency of honeydew elements (HDE) is determined (see 3.5.2.9 and 3.5.2.10), the following terms are used (P = total frequency of pollen grains):
"few" if the quotient HDE/P lies between 0 and 1·5;
"medium quantity" if the quotient HDE/P lies between 1·5 and 3·0;
"numerous", if the quotient HDE/P lies between 3 and 4·5;
"very numerous" if the quotient HDE/P exceeds 4·5.

3.6.2.5 If the frequency of pollen grains of anemophilous and other nectarless plants are quoted, the following terms are used:
"sporadic" if the pollen grains of nectarless plants constitute less than 3 % of the total;
"rare" if the pollen grains of nectarless plants constitute 3–15 % of the total;
"frequent" if the pollen grains of nectarless plants constitute 16–45 % of the total;
"very frequent" if the pollen grains of nectarless pollen grains constitute more than 45 % of the total.

The number of pollen grains of nectarless plants is subtracted before the frequencies of pollens of nectar-producing plants are calculated.

3.7 Interpretation

3.7.1 Geographical origin

In a few cases the geographical origins can be established by the presence of characteristic pollens which are limited to a certain region. More often the presence of certain pollen combinations (honey types) allows a determination of the region in which the honey was produced. Details about characteristic pollens and typical combinations can be found in the literature. The pollen spectrum of a honey is a result of the floral, agricultural and forest conditions of the region in which the honey was produced. Political or administrative frontiers do not denote sudden changes of these conditions. Often, therefore, the microscopical data allow the determination of the geographical region in which the honey was produced rather than the country or state.

3.7.2 Botanical origin

The determination of botanical origin is based on the identification of the pollen grains and other constituents of the sediment and on the frequencies of the different microscopical elements. The frequency of the different pollen grains and honeydew elements allows conclusions as to the extent with which the corresponding honey sources have contributed to the honey in question.

In general a honey has been produced mainly from a certain plant (unifloral honey) if the corresponding pollen is predominant, pollens o anemophilous and nectarless plants being excluded when calculating percentages. This rule is valid only if the honey contains few honeydew elements (quotient HDE/P less than 1). Honeys produced mainly from honeydew contain many honeydew elements (in general HDE/P is 3 or more). The percentage of pollens from nectarless plants is mostly higher than in flower honeys.

3.7.2.1 *Special cases*
The pollen grains of some flowers are over-represented, i.e. the percentage of pollen found in the sediment is greater than the percentage of the corresponding nectar present in the honey. With some other pollens the situation is reversed; they are under-represented.

3.7.2.1.1 *Over-represented pollens*
The most extreme case of over-representation of pollen is *Myosotis* spp. (forget-me-not). If a honey sediment is rich in *Myosotis* pollen, it is therefore recommended to make a second supplementary count excluding *Myosotis*. This revised spectrum gives a better picture of the botanical origin than the normal method of evaluation. The pollen of *Castanea sativa* also belongs to the over-represented constituents of honey sediments. Only honeys containing 90% of pollen from *Castanea* (or more) can be considered to be *Castanea* honey. In sediments with a high percentage of *Castanea* pollen, a second count excluding *Castanea* is recommended (as with *Myosotis*).

In general honeys from flowers with over-represented pollens show a higher absolute pollen content than honeys from sources with normally or under-represented pollens. In doubtful cases it is recommended that the absolute number of microscopic particles should be counted (see 4).

Cynoglossum and *Mimosa pudica* pollens are thought to be over-represented.

3.7.2.1.2 *Under-represented pollens*
The following list gives the most important pollens which are known to be under-represented. If the frequency of these pollens is as high as the percentages listed, the honey is mainly from the corresponding source.

Lavandula spica ✗ *L. latifolia* (lavandin)	10–20%
Salvia (European)	20–30%
Robinia	30%
Tilia	20–30%
Medicago	30%

Chamaenerion, Cucurbitaceae and *Rosmarinus* also belong to the group of under-represented pollens. The anthers of some *Citrus* varieties are almost sterile; there are therefore *Citrus* honeys containing only 10–20% of *Citrus* pollen in the sediment.

In general, honeys from flowers with under-represented pollens show a low absolute number of pollen grains. In doubtful cases a quantitative evaluation should be made (see 4).

3.7.2.1.3 Certain anomalies in representation must be taken into account: plants which produce extrafloral nectar; dioecious plants (whose female individuals do not produce pollen); plants which do not disperse their pollen, e.g. many Orchidaceae and Asclepiadaceae which produce pollinia comprising all the pollen grains from a theca.

3.7.2.1.4 The botanical origin of honeys which contain a high percentage of unknown pollen grains must be treated with reserve, because the degree of representation of these pollen grains is unknown.

3.7.2.1.5 Some unifloral honeys are characterized by specific chemical or physical properties, whose presence may complete and confirm the results of microscopical analysis. Simple methods are available for measuring the thixotropy and the protein content of heather (*Calluna*) honey. Honeydew honeys are characterized by a high electrical conductivity. *Robinia* and tupelo honeys show a high fructose content.

3.8 Reproducibility

Vergeron (1964) has published a paper on the repeatability of pollen-grain counts; these findings were taken into account in compiling the rules for counting described in 3.5.2 and 3.6.2. The reproducibility of counts from preparations of the same honey in different laboratories showed a good conformity.

A "ring-analysis" has not yet been performed systematically. Statistical evaluation of ring-analyses is problematical, because the identification of pollen grains and the result of counting depend on the experience and performance of the operator. A ring-analysis may therefore give more information about the analyst's competence than about the reproducibility of the method.

4. QUANTITATIVE MICROSCOPICAL ANALYSIS

4.1 Determination of the amount of sediment in honey

4.1.1 Scope

The determination of sediment is, strictly speaking, not a microscopical procedure; it should, nevertheless, be described here, since the result of the determination shows whether or not certain methods of evaluation are admissible (see 2.2).

4.1.1.1 Determination of sediment provides information about the method of honey extraction (pressing, centrifuging, straining) and

4.1.1.2 about any contamination with large numbers of particles not usually present in honey (of dirt, pollen substitutes, yeasts, etc.).

4.1.2 Field of application

The determination of the amount of sediment is possible with all honeys.

4.1.3 Principle

Sedimentation of water-insoluble matter by centrifugation of honey solution. Measurement of the sediment in calibrated centrifuge tubes.

4.1.4 Apparatus

Centrifuge tubes ca. 50-ml capacity (see 3.3)
Centrifuge (see 3.3)
Water-operated or other vacuum pump
Centrifuge tubes about 10-ml capacity with a calibrated tubular end; capacity of the calibrated part 0·2 ml, graduation 0·01 ml (*Trommsdorfröhrchen*).

4.1.5 Samples (see 3.4)

4.1.6 Procedure

10 g of honey are weighed to 0·01 g and dissolved in 20 ml hot water (not above 40°C). The solution is centrifuged for 10 min and the supernatant liquid drawn off carefully, so that a fluid column 1–2 cm remains above the sediment.

8

The sediment is dispersed and poured quantitatively into a small calibrated centrifuge tube of appropriate capacity and centrifuged again for 10 min. If the sediment is extremely high or extremely low the quantity of honey may be halved or doubled respectively. The tubular calibrated end of the centrifuge tube should be protected by a suitable piece of vacuum rubber tube or a metal tube during centrifugation.

4.1.7 Results and evaluation

The amount of sediment is measured from the graduated end of the tube. Honeys extracted by centrifugation contain little sediment. In general, from 10 g of honey 0·015–0·035 ml of insoluble matter is obtained. More than 0·1 ml of sediment indicates a pressed honey, unless most of the sediment is due to material not usually present in honey (dirt, pollen substitutes, yeasts, etc.). Low amounts of sediment indicate honeys naturally poor in pollen (e.g. orange), but may also indicate excessive filtering or falsification (e.g. by sugar feeding).

4.2 Determination of the absolute number of plant elements in honey

4.2.1 Scope

Determination of the absolute number of plant elements in a given quantity of honey.

4.2.2 Field of application

Applicable to all honeys.

4.2.3 Determination according to Maurizio

4.2.3.1 *Principle*

Concentration of the sediment of a given quantity of honey. Dispersion of the sediment in a known volume of water. Spreading a known volume of the dispersion over a circumscribed surface of a slide. Counting the microscopic elements and calculating the number per unit weight.

4.2.3.2 *Apparatus*

Erlenmeyer flasks marked at 100 ml
Centrifuge tubes 10-ml capacity, calibrated
Centrifuge tubes, 100-ml capacity (with conical ends)
Centrifuge (see 3.3)
Breed-pipettes 0·01-ml, calibrated
Slides
Microscope (magnification about 300×) with a mechanical stage and an eyepiece with a graticule.

4.2.3.3 *Samples* (see 3.4)

4.2.3.4 *Procedure*

4.2.3.4.1 *Preparation of slides*

2 portions of honey, 50 g each, are weighed in separate Erlenmeyer flasks. The honey is dissolved in a water-bath and the flask filled up to 100 ml. For honeys rich in sediment, 2 portions each 10–30 g are sufficient. The honey solution is centrifuged in tubes of 100-ml capacity. The supernatant liquid

is cautiously decanted, the sediment dispersed with a platinum rod and transferred quantitatively to a 10-ml calibrated centrifuge tube by rinsing the large tube several times with distilled water. The dispersion is centrifuged again for 5 min, the supernatant solution decanted or drawn off, and the sediment dispersed in a volume of water appropriate to the quantity of sediment. This will give a convenient concentration of the plant constituents (see statistical evaluations, Maurizio, 1939). In general, a dispersion volume of 0·5 ml gives a suitable concentration of sediments obtained from 50 g honey extracted centrifugally. For honeys rich in sediment, a dispersion volume of 1 ml or more is recommended.

The sediment is stirred with a platinum rod. Using a calibrated Breed-pipette, 0·01 ml of the dispersion is transferred to a slide, blown out and spread to a surface of 1 cm^2, the area having previously been traced out beneath the slide. On each slide 2 drops of the same dispersion are spread out into smears side by side. Altogether 4 smear preparations are made, 2 sediment dispersions having been prepared from each honey. The smears are dried. A kind of glaze is formed by the sugars remaining in the dispersion which allows microscopic examination without a cover-glass.

4.2.3.4.2 *Counting of plant constituents*
Counting is done at a magnification of 300 ×, by means of a graticule. In each smear, 100 fields of view are counted, starting from the middle of one side and progressing to the opposite side, displacing the field of view by the mechanical stage. This allows identical examinations of the edges and of the centre of the preparation.

In each field of view, pollen grains, fungus spores and algae are counted and noted separately.

4.2.3.5 *Calculation and interpretation*
The calculation of the absolute number of pollen grains, fungus spores and algae is based on the average number in the 400 fields of view, the surface of a field of view, the dispersion volume, and the quantity of honey used. The result is expressed as the number of plant elements in 1 g or 10 g of honey.

Experience shows that the absolute number of plant constituents in unifloral honeys poor in pollen grains (e.g. *Robinia* honey or *Citrus* honey) lies in general below 20 000 in 10 g (group I). The majority of flower honeys and mixed flower-honeydew honeys shows an absolute number of particles between 20 000 and 100 000 (group II). In group III, with an absolute number of 100 000–500 000 plant elements, are honeydew honeys, and flower honeys rich in pollen (*Myosotis* and *Castanea*). Group IV, with 500 000–1 000 000 plant constituents, comprises flower honeys extremely rich in pollen and some pressed honeys. Group V, with more than 1 000 000 plant constituents, includes only pressed honeys rich in pollen.

The result of counting is expressed by a formula. For example, 32/38/0.7—II means 32 000 pollen grains, 38 000 fungus spores, and 700 algae cells in 10 g of honey. With 70 700 plant constituents in 10 g, the honey belongs to group II. In this case, the formula shows a mixed honey, from nectar and honeydew sources. A floral honey would show e.g. 28/1/0—II. The results are usually expressed in terms of 10 g of honey, since this is the standard quantity for microscopical examination. The result could alternatively be expressed as the number of plant constituents in 1 g of honey.

4.2.4 *Determination according to Demianowicz*
4.2.4.1 *Principle* (see 4.2.3.1)
4.2.4.2 *Apparatus* (see 4.2.3.2)
4.2.4.3 *Samples* (see 3.4)
4.2.4.4 *Procedure*
4.2.4.4.1 *Preparation of slides*
4.2.4.4.1.1 *Experimentally obtained single-species honey**
A drop of undiluted honey is placed on a previously weighed cover-glass, and the glass reweighed. The cover-glass is then inverted and placed on a microscope slide. The amount of honey must be chosen so that none is squeezed out beyond the edge of the cover-glass.

4.2.4.4.1.2 *Unifloral honeys**
The preparation is as described by Maurizio. Demianowicz recommends drawing squares (1-cm side) on the slide, with Indian ink. The Indian ink keeps the sediment dispersion from flowing out of the prescribed square.

4.2.4.4.2 *Counting*
Instead of counting 100 fields of view per smear, plant constituents are counted in strips across the preparation. The number of strips depends on the absolute number of particles in the honey. If the number of plant constituents is below 12 000, 8 strips should be counted; if it is between 12 000 and 96 000, 4 strips should be counted. With 96 000, 2 strips are sufficient. From the numbers obtained by counting strips, the number of plant constituents per square centimetre is calculated, and from this result the absolute number per unit weight of honey.

4.2.4.5 *Interpretation* (see 4.2.3.5)

4.2.5 *Determination according to Louveaux*
4.2.5.1 *Principle of the method*
Separation of sediment of a weighed quantity of honey. Dispersion of the sediment with water and filtering through a filter of known surface area and a pore width less than the diameter of the particles to be counted. Clearing of the filter after drying, with immersion oil. Counting of the elements retained on the filter under the microscope. Calculation of the number of particles per unit of weight, based on the surface of the field of view, the number of fields of view, the number of elements counted, the surface of the filter and the quantity of honey used.

4.2.5.2 *Reagents*
Immersion oil Millipore, refractive index 1·515.

4.2.5.3 *Apparatus*
Centrifuge tubes 50-ml capacity and centrifuge (see 3.3)
Water-operated vacuum pump or another device to draw off solutions
Pyrex-micro-filtration apparatus of the Millipore-Filter-Corporation (XX 10 025 00)

---

* In this text a "unifloral honey" means normally obtained extracted honey, mostly from a single plant species (see 3.7.2). The term "single-species honey" is reserved for honey from bees allowed to forage on one flowering species only, and known from experimental conditions to have access to no other source of food.

11

Filter 25 mm diameter, white, smooth, width of pores ca 1μ
Microscope (see 3.3)
Slides at least 2·5 cm wide

4.2.5.4 *Samples* (see 3.4)

4.2.5.5 *Procedure*

4.2.5.5.1 *Preparation*

A quantity of honey is weighed to 1 mg. Usually 10 g is an appropriate quantity. In the case of honeys very poor in pollen, 20 g may be used; if the honey is rich in pollen, less than 10 g, as too many pollen grains in the field of view render counting difficult. The honey is dissolved in 20 ml of distilled water (preferably hot, but not above 40°C) and centrifuged for 10 min. The supernatant fluid is drawn off. A liquid column of about 2 cm is left above the sediment. The tube is filled again with distilled water and centrifuged again. After drawing off the supernatant solution as described below, the sediment is dispersed in about 10 ml distilled water and put into the cylindrical upper part of the filtration apparatus. By means of a slight vacuum the dispersion is drawn through the Millipore filter. Addition of a drop of a detergent solution facilitates this operation. The centrifuge tube is rinsed several times with distilled water, which is filtered too. In order to obtain a uniform sedimentation on the filter, turbulence must be avoided when new portions of liquid are put into the cylinder. Finally the sides of the cylinder are washed before the filter dries. The filter is taken out of the apparatus and dried by slight warming. The cylinder is thoroughly washed with a detergent solution. Some drops of immersion oil are put on a slide and covered with the filter, which becomes clear and translucent; 1 or 2 additional drops are put on the upper surface and the preparation enclosed with a cover glass.

4.2.5.5.2 *Counting and evaluation*

The plant constituents are counted in 100 fields of view at a magnification 800 ×. The rim and the central part of the filter should be given identical observation. The diameter of filter surface used can in general be identified without difficulty because the plant constituents give it a slightly yellow or brownish colour. By straining a solution of Indian ink through the filter the surface used can be measured easily. The number of microscopic elements in the quantity of honey prepared is given by the formula:

$$N = (F \times n) / (f \times a)$$

N = total number of elements in the quantity of honey prepared
F = used surface of the filter in mm²
f = field of view in mm²
n = number of elements counted
a = number of fields of view counted.

4.2.5.5.3 *Evaluation* (see 4.2.3.5)

4.2.6 *Reproducibility*

A ring-analysis between different laboratories with the methods mentioned has not yet been performed. A paper concerned with repeatability (as worked out by Vergeron) for counting the relative percentages of pollens is not available. Nevertheless, good conformity was obtained when counts were made on similar honeys in different laboratories.

5. PREPARATION OF REFERENCE SLIDES

5.1 Purpose

A collection of reference preparations is a valuable supplement to the literature on melissopalynology.

5.2 Reagents

Diethyl ether analytical grade
Fuchsine (NB) powder
Fuchsine solution, alcoholic 0·1 %
Kaiser's glycerine gelatine.

5.3 Samples

Flowers of identified plants (fresh or dry). Zander recommends collecting the flower as buds and letting them open in the laboratory. Open flowers out of doors are often contaminated with pollen of other plants by wind or by visits of insects.

5.4 Procedure

5.4.1 Unstained preparations of degreased pollen

The anthers, the whole flowers or inflorescences, are washed out in a watchglass filled with ether. The ether is decanted, and the pollen rinsed with fresh ether which is also decanted. After drying the pollen is transferred to a slide and spread out. The preparation is dried, preferably by slight warming (not over 40°C), and mounted with glycerine gelatine. If the pollen grains are slow in swelling, the preparation is kept warm until an appropriate degree of swelling is obtained.

If the pollens have a tendency to burst, the fat is removed from them with ether directly on the slide. The pollen is mounted quickly, with minimal warming.

5.4.2 Unstained preparations without removal of fat

Pollen is stripped off the flowers or anthers with a microscope slide, or ripe anthers are emptied on to a slide with needles. The pollen is spread out, and remains of anthers and any dirt particles removed. The preparation is then mounted with glycerine gelatine.

5.4.3 Stained degreased preparations

Preparation as described under 5.4.1. Instead of unstained gelatine, a stained mounting material is used. Stained gelatine is prepared by adding some drops of alcoholic fuchsine solution to melted glycerine gelatine. Pollens show different affinities to fuchsine, some being stained easily, others slowly. The preparation of a set of glycerine gelatine specimens with different concentrations of fuchsine is recommended, by adding 0·2–1·5 ml alcoholic solution to 10 ml liquefied glycerine gelatine.

13

5.5 Stability of preparations

The pollen grains in reference preparations alter in the course of time. If the fatty oil was not removed from them, it becomes pale. Also the exine loses colour. In all types of preparation the diameter of pollen grains increases with time, because of swelling. Old preparations are not useless, as they sometimes show particular characteristics better than fresh ones, but they should not be used for the comparison of diameters. It is therefore best to complete the collection from time to time with new preparations. The cover glasses may be sealed with Caedax, liquid Canada balsam or a suitable lacquer.

In hot and humid climates, preparations are ruined because the gelatine melts and gets mouldy. In order to protect the collection, it should be stored in refrigerator or cool-room. Sealing with paraffin wax (Erdtman, 1966, 1969), is advantageous.

The pollen is spread over a restricted area and covered with a small quantity glycerine gelatine so that the mounting medium does not reach the edges of the cover-glass. Paraffin wax is melted in a porcelain crucible. Some drops are transferred with a glass rod to the edge of the cover glass. If the slide was slightly warmed beforehand, the wax spreads into the gap between cover-glass and slide and seals the preparation hermetically. The gelatine is prevented from flowing out even if it becomes liquid, and is protected against moulds.

6. LITERATURE

ARMBRUSTER, L. & OENIKE, G. (1929) Die Pollenformen als Mittel zur Honigherkunftsbestimmung. *Neumünster : Wachholtz*
ARMBRUSTER, L. & JACOBS, J. (1934/1935) Pollenformen und Honigherkunftsbestimmung. *Arch. Bienenk.* 15(8) : 227–308; 16(1, 2/3) : 17–106
BEUG, H. J. (1961) Leitfaden der Pollenbestimmung. 1 Lfg *Stuttgart : Fischer*
BROWN, C. A. (1960) Palynological techniques. *Baton Rouge*
DEMIANOWICZ, Z. (1961) Pollenkoeffizienten als Grundlage der quantitativen Pollenanalyse des Honigs. *Pszczel. Zesz. nauk.* 5(2) : 95–105
―――― (1964) Charakteristik der Einartenhonige. *Annls Abeille* 7(4) : 273–288
ERDTMAN, G. (1966) Pollen morphology and plant taxonomy. I. Angiosperms. Off-set edition with addendum. *New York : Hafner*
―――― (1969) Handbook of palynology. *Copenhagen : Munksgaard*
EVENIUS, J. & FOCKE, E. (1967) Mikroskopische Untersuchung des Honigs. Handbuch der Lebensmittelchemie. Bd. 5, Teil 1. p. 560–590 *Berlin : Springer*
FAEGRI, K. & IVERSEN, J. (1964) Textbook of modern pollen analysis. 2nd ed. *Copenhagen : Munksgaard*
GENIER, G. (1966) Le pollen des Ericaceae dans les miels français. *Annls Abeille* 9(4) : 271–321
GONTARSKI, H. (1951) Zur Frage der Formbestandteile des Waldhonigs. *Z. Bienenforsch.* 1(3) : 33–37
GRIEBEL, C. (1930, 1931) Zur Pollenanalyse des Honigs. *Z. Unters. Lebensmittel* 59(1) : 63–79, (2/3) : 197–211, (5) : 441–471; 61(3) : 241–306
HYDE, H. A. & ADAMS, K. F. (1958) An atlas of airborne pollen grains. *London : Macmillan*
INTERNATIONALE KOMMISSION FÜR BIENENBOTANIK DER I.U.B.S. (1962/1963) Methodik der Honig-Pollenanalyse. *Z. Bienenforsch.* 6(4) : 115–116; *Bee Wld* 43(4) : 122–124; *Annls Abeille* 6(1) : 75–76
LOUVEAUX, J. (1961) Techniques améliorées pour l'analyse pollinique des miels. *Z. Bienenforsch.* 5(7) : 199–204
―――― (1966) Essai de caractérisation des miels de callune (*Calluna vulgaris* Salisb.). *Annls Abeille* 9(4) : 351–358

14

——— (1968) L'analyse pollinique des miels. III, pages 325–362, "Traité de biologie de l'abeille" ed. R. Chauvin *Paris : Masson*

LOUVEAUX, J. & VERGERON, P. (1964) Étude du spectre pollinique de quelques miels espagnols. *Annls Abeille* 7(4) : 329–347

MAURIZIO, A. (1939) Untersuchungen zur quantitativen Pollenanalyse des Honigs. *Mitt. Geb. Lebensmittelunters. u. Hyg.* 30(1/2) : 27–69

——— (1949) Beiträge zur quantitativen Pollenanalyse des Honigs. *Beih. Schweiz. Bienenztg* 2(18) : 320–421

——— (1955) Beiträge zur quantitativen Pollenanalyse des Honigs. 2. Absoluter Gehalt pflanzlicher Bestandteile in Tilia- und Labiaten-Honigen. *Z. Bienenforsch.* 3(2) : 32–39

——— (1958) Beiträge zur quantitativen Pollenanalyse des Honigs. 3. Absoluter Gehalt pflanzlicher Bestandteile in Esparsette-, Luzerne-, Orangen- und Rapshonigen. *Annls Abeille* 1(2) : 93–106

——— (1959) Zur Frage der Mikroskopie von Honigtauhonig. *Annls Abeille* 2(2) : 145–157

——— (1966) Das Pollenbild europäischer Heidehonige. *Annls Abeille* 9(4) : 375–387

MAURIZIO, A. & LOUVEAUX, J. (1965) Pollen de plantes mellifères d'Europe. *Paris : Union des Groupements apicoles français*

——— (1967) Les méthodes et la terminologie en mélissopalynologie. *Rev. Palaeobot. Palynol.* 3 : 291–295

VAN CAMPO, M. (1954) Considérations générales sur les caractères des pollens et des spores et sur leur diagnose. *Bull. Soc. bot. Fr.* 101(5/6) : 250–281

VERGERON, P. (1964) Interprétation statistique des résultats en matière d'analyse pollinique des miels. *Annls Abeille* 7(4) : 349–364

VORWOHL, G. (1964) Die Beziehungen zwischen der elektrischen Leitfähigkeit der Honige und ihrer trachtmässigen Herkunft. *Annls Abeille* 7(4) : 301–309

——— (1966) Das mikroskopische Bild der Pollenersatzmittel und des Sediments von Futterteigen. *Z. Bienenforsch.* 8(5) : 222–228

——— (1968a) Grundzüge einer modernen Pollenbeschreibung im Rahmen der Bienen- und Honigkunde. *Z. Bienenforsch.* 9(5) : 224–230

——— (1968b) Bericht über die Diskussion der Auswertungsverfahren und über die Terminologie der mikroskopischen Honiguntersuchung. *Z. Bienenforsch.* 9(5) : 230–231

ZANDER, E. (1935, 1937, 1941, 1949, 1951) Beiträge zur Herkunftsbestimmung bei Honig. I *Berlin : Reichsfachgruppe Imker;* II, III, V *Leipzig : Liedloff, Loth & Michaelis;* IV *München : Ehrenwirth*

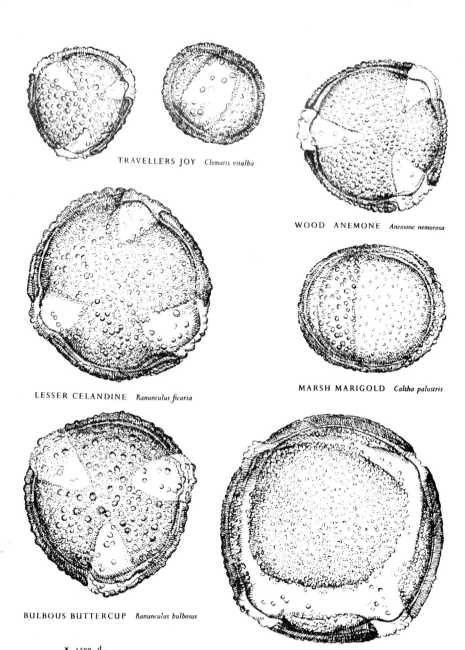

TRAVELLERS JOY *Clematis vitalba*

WOOD ANEMONE *Anemone nemorosa*

LESSER CELANDINE *Ranunculus ficaria*

MARSH MARIGOLD *Caltha palustris*

BULBOUS BUTTERCUP *Ranunculus bulbosus*

x 1500 d.

20 microns

BERBERIS *Mahonia aquifolia*

RANUNCULACEAE BERBERIDACEAE

I

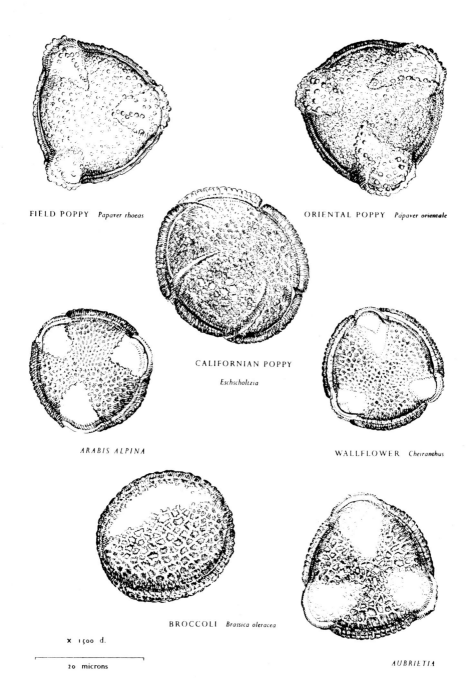

FIELD POPPY *Papaver rhoeas*

ORIENTAL POPPY *Papaver orientale*

CALIFORNIAN POPPY

Eschscholtzia

ARABIS ALPINA

WALLFLOWER *Cheiranthus*

BROCCOLI *Brassica oleracea*

X 1500 d.

20 microns

AUBRIETIA

PAPAVERACEAE CRUCIFERAE

2

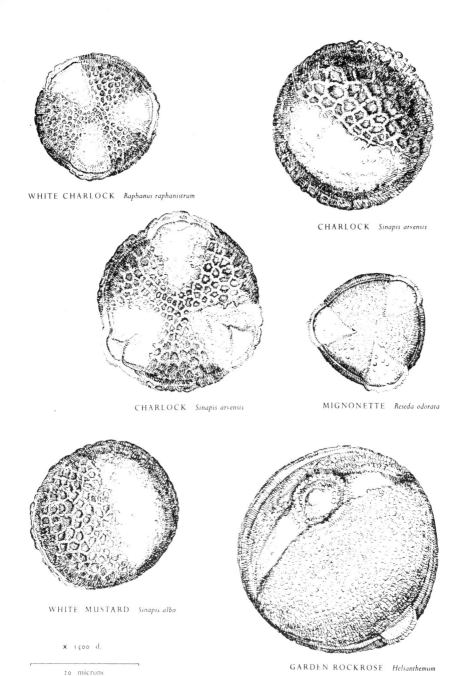

WHITE CHARLOCK   *Raphanus raphanistrum*

CHARLOCK   *Sinapis arvensis*

CHARLOCK   *Sinapis arvensis*

MIGNONETTE   *Reseda odorata*

WHITE MUSTARD   *Sinapis alba*

x 1500 d.

20 microns

GARDEN ROCKROSE   *Helianthemum*

CRUCIFERAE RESEDACEAE CISTACEAE

3

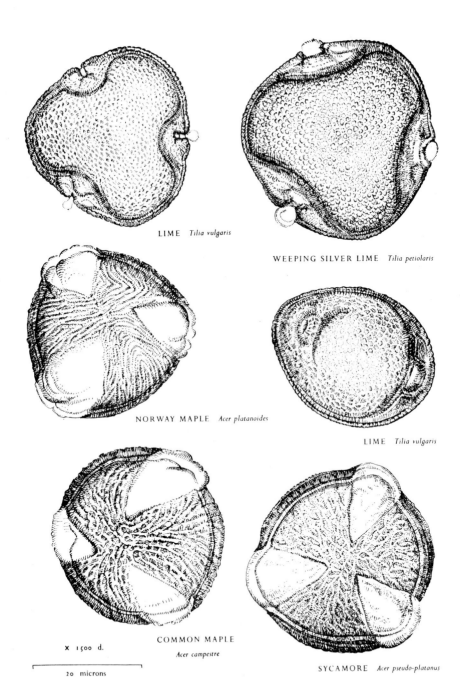

LIME *Tilia vulgaris*

WEEPING SILVER LIME *Tilia petiolaris*

NORWAY MAPLE *Acer platanoides*

LIME *Tilia vulgaris*

x 1500 d.

20 microns

COMMON MAPLE
Acer campestre

SYCAMORE *Acer pseudo-platanus*

TILIACEAE ACERACEAE

4

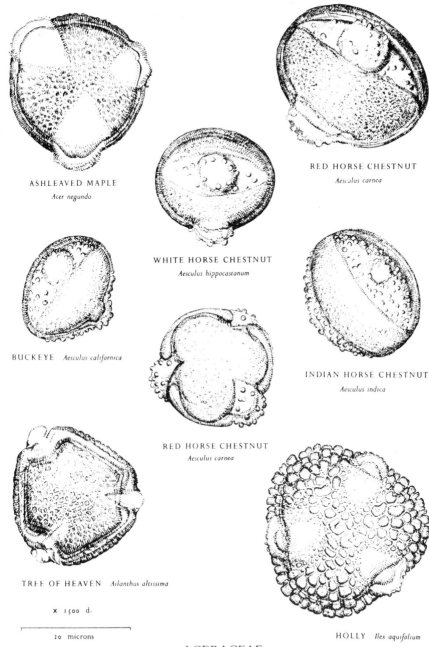

ASHLEAVED MAPLE
Acer negundo

RED HORSE CHESTNUT
Aesculus carnea

WHITE HORSE CHESTNUT
Aesculus hippocastanum

BUCKEYE *Aesculus californica*

INDIAN HORSE CHESTNUT
Aesculus indica

RED HORSE CHESTNUT
Aesculus carnea

TREE OF HEAVEN *Ailanthus altissima*

x 1500 d.

20 microns

HOLLY *Ilex aquifolium*

ACERACEAE
HIPPOCASTANACEAE AQUIFOLIACEAE SIMARUBACEAE

5

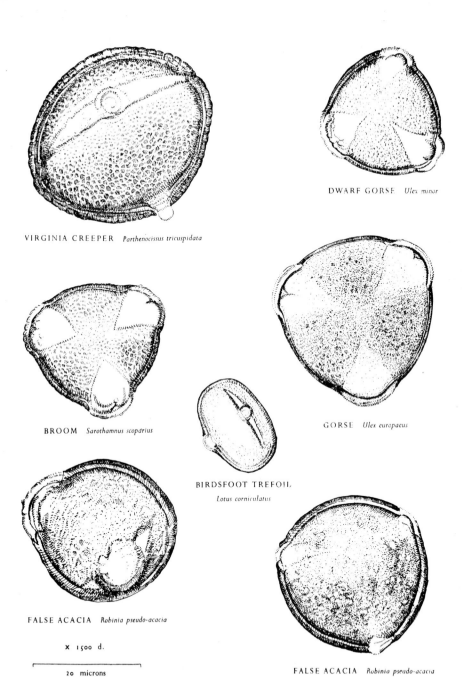

VIRGINIA CREEPER *Parthenocissus tricuspidata*

DWARF GORSE *Ulex minor*

BROOM *Sarothamnus scoparius*

BIRDSFOOT TREFOIL
Lotus corniculatus

GORSE *Ulex europaeus*

FALSE ACACIA *Robinia pseudo-acacia*

x 1500 d.

20 microns

FALSE ACACIA *Robinia pseudo-acacia*

RHAMNACEAE   LEGUMINOSAE

6

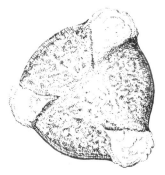

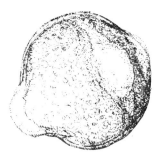

WHITE CLOVER *Trifolium repens*

WHITE CLOVER *Trifolium repens*

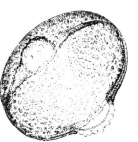

ALSIKE CLOVER
Trifolium hybridum

YELLOW MELILOT *Melilotus officinalis*

WHITE MELILOT *Melilotus alba*

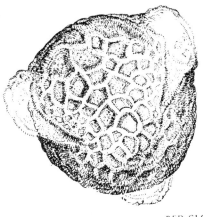

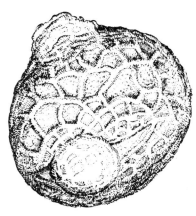

x 1500 d.

RED CLOVER
Trifolium pratense

20 microns

RED·CLOVER *Trifolium pratense*

LEGUMINOSAE

7

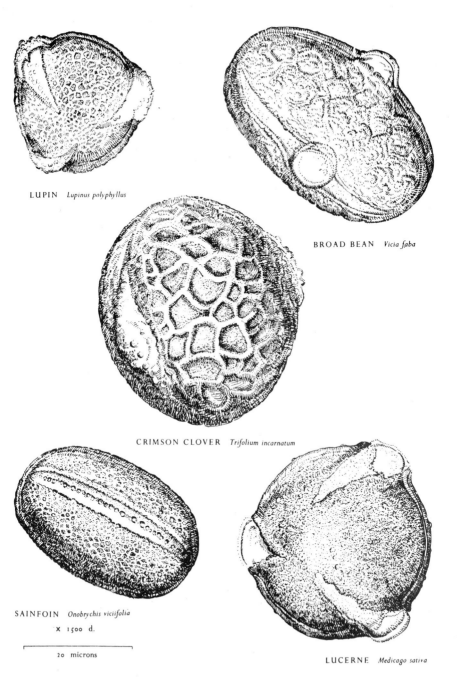

LUPIN   *Lupinus polyphyllus*

BROAD BEAN   *Vicia faba*

CRIMSON CLOVER   *Trifolium incarnatum*

SAINFOIN   *Onobrychis viciifolia*

x 1500 d.

20 microns

LUCERNE   *Medicago sativa*

LEGUMINOSAE

8

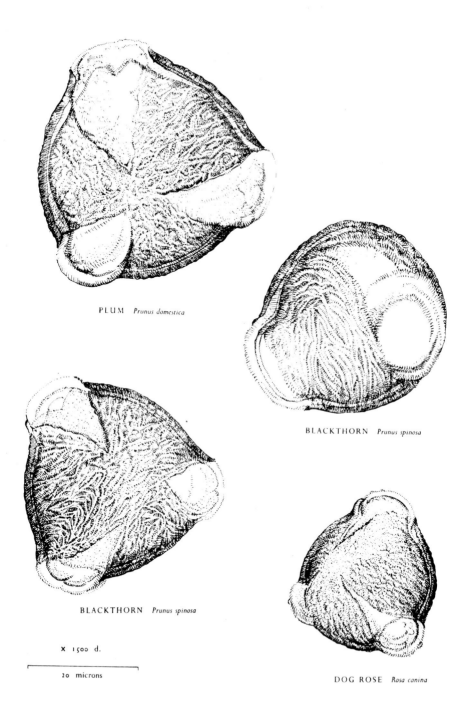

PLUM   *Prunus domestica*

BLACKTHORN   *Prunus spinosa*

BLACKTHORN   *Prunus spinosa*

✕ 1500 d.

20 microns

DOG ROSE   *Rosa canina*

ROSACEAE

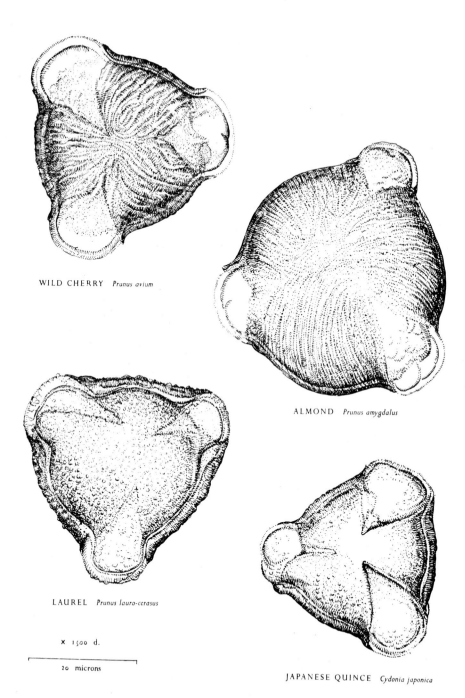

WILD CHERRY *Prunus avium*

ALMOND *Prunus amygdalus*

LAUREL *Prunus lauro-cerasus*

× 1500 d.

20 microns

JAPANESE QUINCE *Cydonia japonica*

ROSACEAE

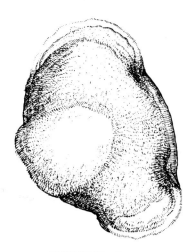

HAWTHORN *Crataegus monogyna*

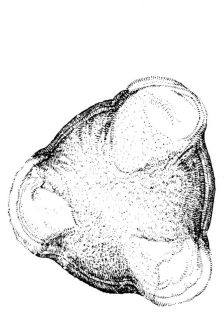

HAWTHORN *Crataegus monogyna*

APPLE *Malus pumila*

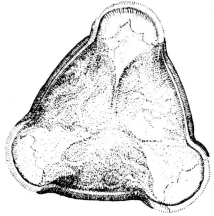

APPLE *Malus pumila*

× 1500 d.

20 microns

ROSACEAE

I I

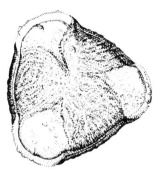

RASPBERRY *Rubus idaeus*

RASPBERRY *Rubus idaeus*

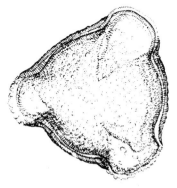

BLACKBERRY *Rubus fruticosus*

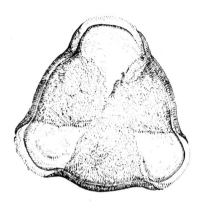

PEAR *Pyrus communis*

MEADOWSWEET *Filipendula ulmaria*

x 1500 d.

20 microns

MOUNTAIN ASH *Sorbus aucuparia*

ROSACEAE

12

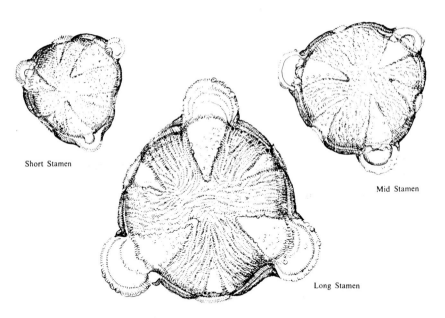

Short Stamen

Mid Stamen

Long Stamen

PURPLE LOOSESTRIFE *Lythrum salicaria*

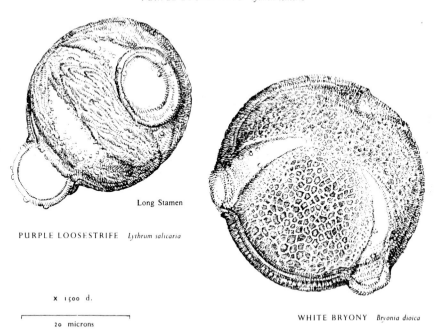

Long Stamen

PURPLE LOOSESTRIFE *Lythrum salicaria*

x 1500 d.

20 microns

WHITE BRYONY *Bryonia dioica*

LYTHRACEAE   CUCURBITACEAE

13

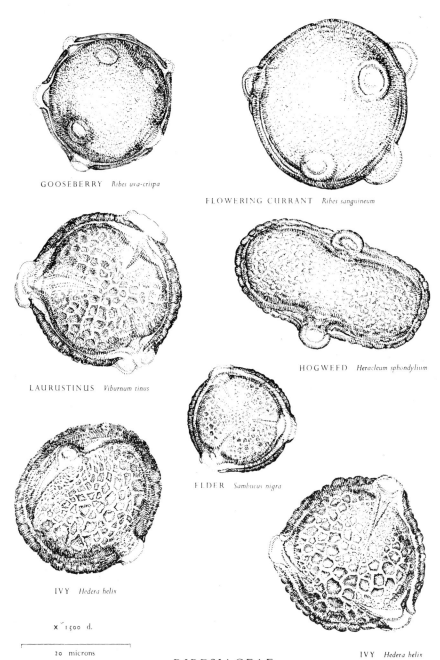

GOOSEBERRY   *Ribes uva-crispa*

FLOWERING CURRANT   *Ribes sanguineum*

LAURUSTINUS   *Viburnum tinus*

HOGWEED   *Heracleum sphondylium*

ELDER   *Sambucus nigra*

IVY   *Hedera helix*

x 1500 d.

20 microns

IVY   *Hedera helix*

RIBESIACEAE
UMBELLIFERAE CAPRIFOLIACEAE ARALIACEAE

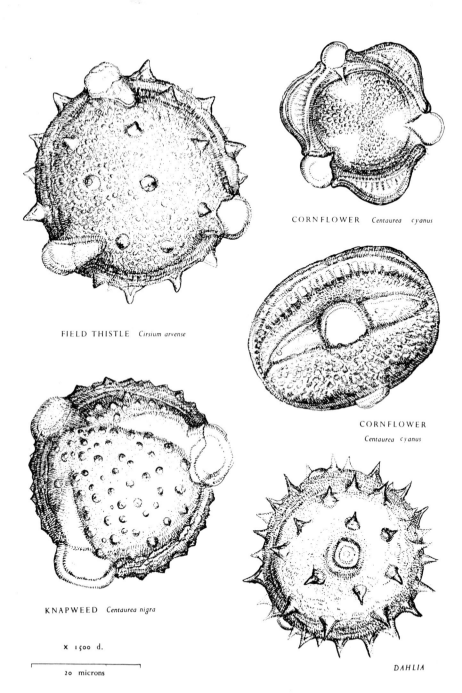

FIELD THISTLE *Cirsium arvense*

CORNFLOWER *Centaurea cyanus*

CORNFLOWER
Centaurea cyanus

KNAPWEED *Centaurea nigra*

X 1500 d.

20 microns

DAHLIA

COMPOSITAE

15

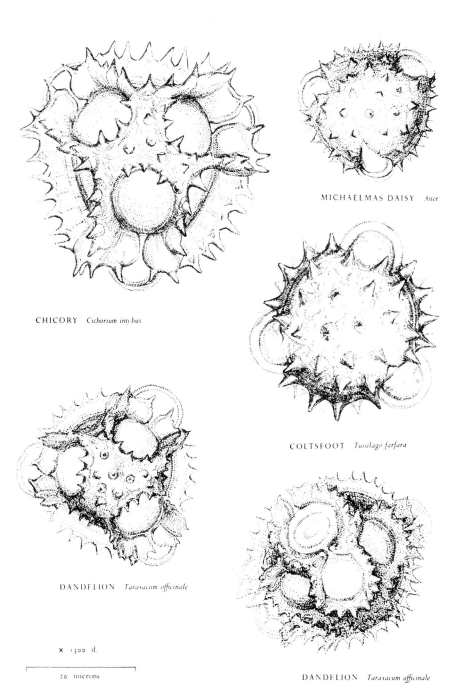

MICHAELMAS DAISY   *Aster*

CHICORY   *Cichorium intybus*

COLTSFOOT   *Tussilago farfara*

DANDELION   *Taraxacum officinale*

x 1500 d.

20 microns

DANDELION   *Taraxacum officinale*

COMPOSITAE

16

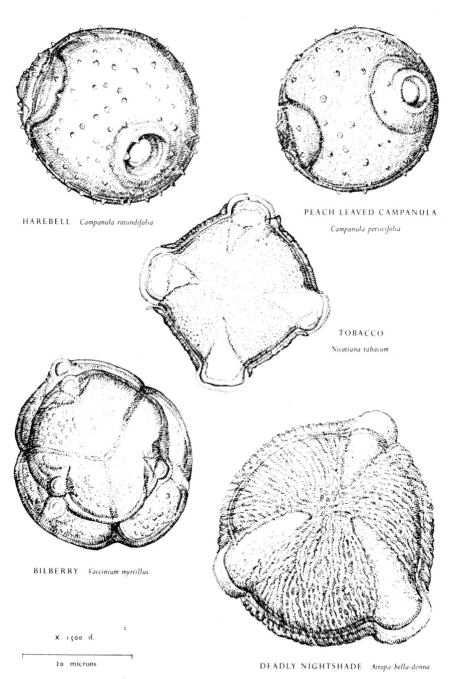

HAREBELL *Campanula rotundifolia*

PEACH LEAVED CAMPANULA
Campanula persicifolia

TOBACCO
Nicotiana tabacum

BILBERRY *Vaccinium myrtillus*

x 1500 d.

20 microns

DEADLY NIGHTSHADE *Atropa bella-donna*

CAMPANULACEAE SOLANACEAE ERICACEAE

17

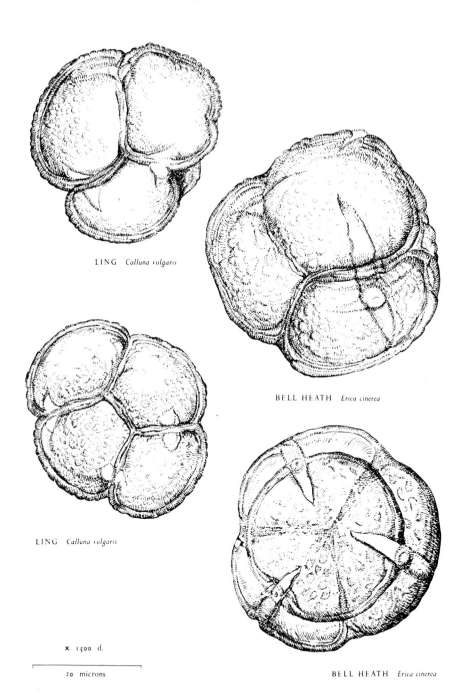

LING   *Calluna vulgaris*

BELL HEATH   *Erica cinerea*

LING   *Calluna vulgaris*

× 1500 d.

20 microns

BELL HEATH   *Erica cinerea*

ERICACEAE

18

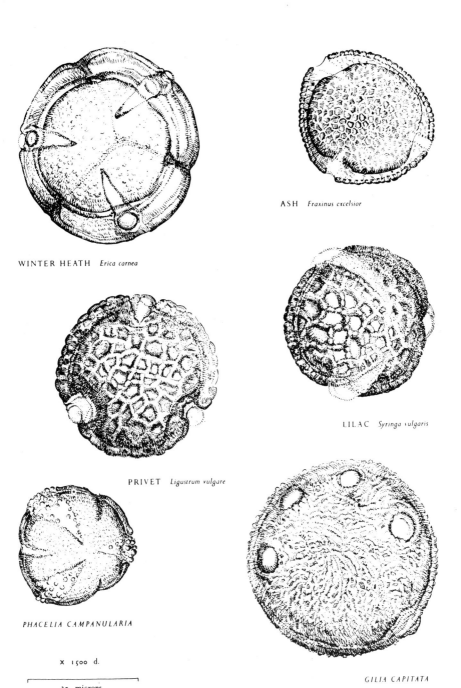

WINTER HEATH   *Erica carnea*

ASH   *Fraxinus excelsior*

PRIVET   *Ligustrum vulgare*

LILAC   *Syringa vulgaris*

PHACELIA CAMPANULARIA

x 1500 d.

20 microns

GILIA CAPITATA

ERICACEAE OLEACEAE POLEMONIACEAE HYDROPHYLLACEAE

19

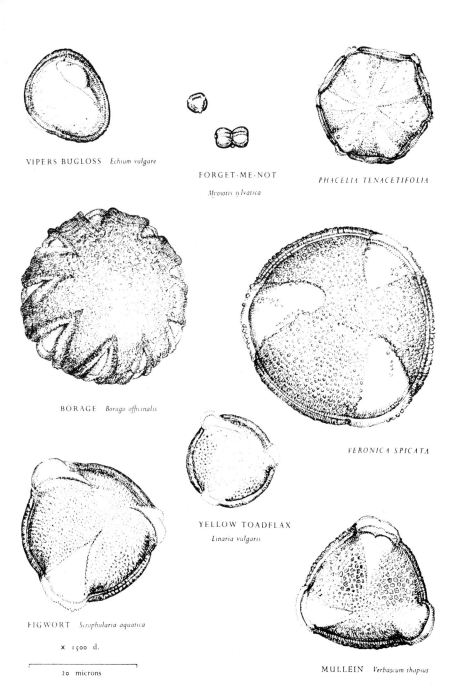

VIPERS BUGLOSS   *Echium vulgare*

FORGET-ME-NOT

Myosotis sylvatica

PHACELIA TENACETIFOLIA

BORAGE   *Borago officinalis*

VERONICA SPICATA

YELLOW TOADFLAX

Linaria vulgaris

FIGWORT   *Scrophularia aquatica*

x 1500 d.

20 microns

MULLEIN   *Verbascum thapsus*

HYDROPHYLLACEAE BORAGINACEAE SCROPHULARIACEAE

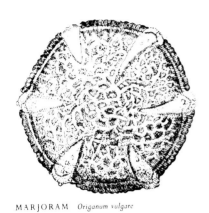

MARJORAM *Origanum vulgare*

MARJORAM *Origanum vulgare*

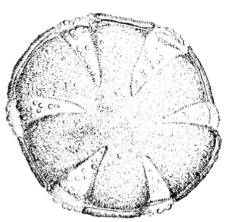

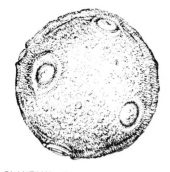

RED DEADNETTLE *Lamium purpureum*

ROSEMARY *Rosmarinus officinalis*

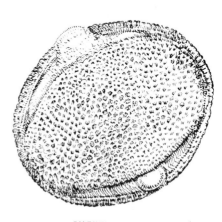

PLANTAIN *Plantago*

x 1500 d.

20 microns

BUCKWHEAT *Fagopyrum esculentum*

LABIATAE PLANTAGINACEAE POLYGONACEAE

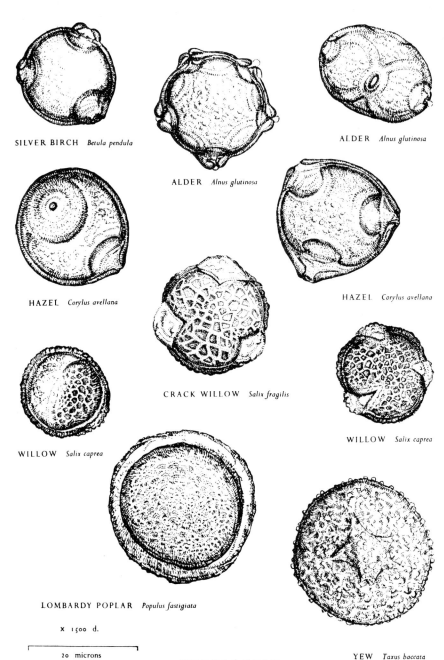

SILVER BIRCH *Betula pendula*

ALDER *Alnus glutinosa*

ALDER *Alnus glutinosa*

HAZEL *Corylus avellana*

HAZEL *Corylus avellana*

CRACK WILLOW *Salix fragilis*

WILLOW *Salix caprea*

WILLOW *Salix caprea*

LOMBARDY POPLAR *Populus fastigiata*

x 1500 d.

20 microns

YEW *Taxus baccata*

CORYLACEAE
BETULACEAE SALICACEAE TAXACEAE

22

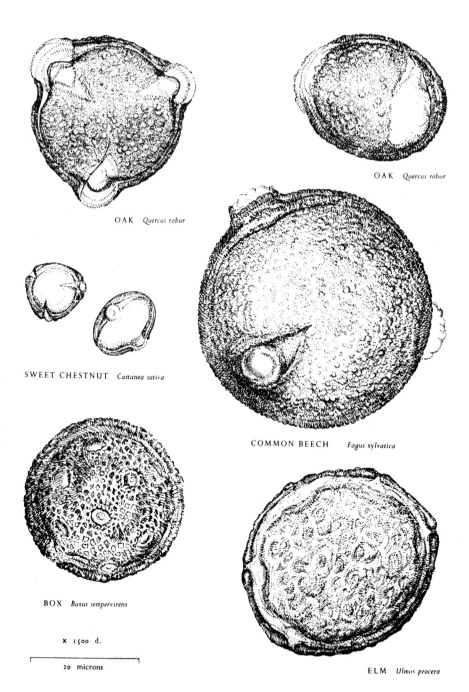

OAK   *Quercus robur*

OAK   *Quercus robur*

SWEET CHESTNUT   *Castanea sativa*

COMMON BEECH   *Fagus sylvatica*

BOX   *Buxus sempervirens*

x 1500 d.

20 microns

ELM   *Ulmus procera*

ULMACEAE EUPHORBIACEAE FAGACEAE

23

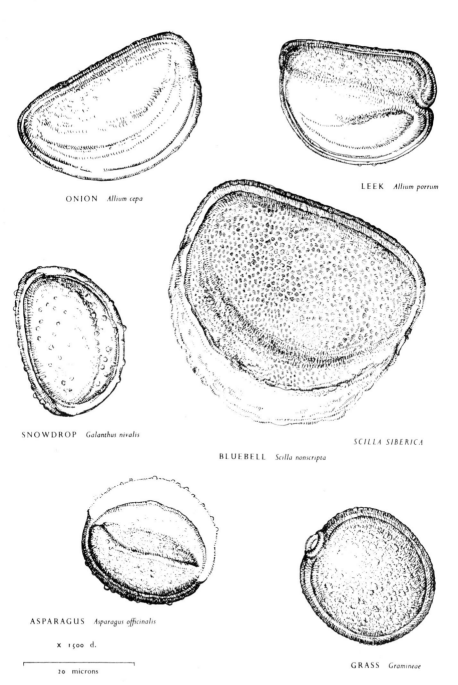

ONION *Allium cepa*

LEEK *Allium porrum*

SNOWDROP *Galanthus nivalis*

BLUEBELL *Scilla nonscripta*

SCILLA SIBERICA

ASPARAGUS *Asparagus officinalis*

x 1500 d.

20 microns

GRASS *Gramineae*

LILIACEAE AMARYLLIDACEAE GRAMINEAE

24

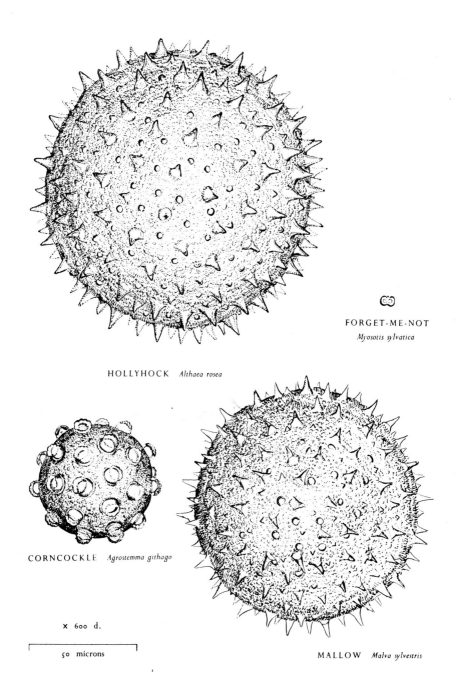

FORGET-ME-NOT
Myosotis sylvatica

HOLLYHOCK *Althaea rosea*

CORNCOCKLE *Agrostemma githago*

x 600 d.

50 microns

MALLOW *Malva sylvestris*

MALVACEAE CARYOPHYLLACEAE BORAGINACEAE

25

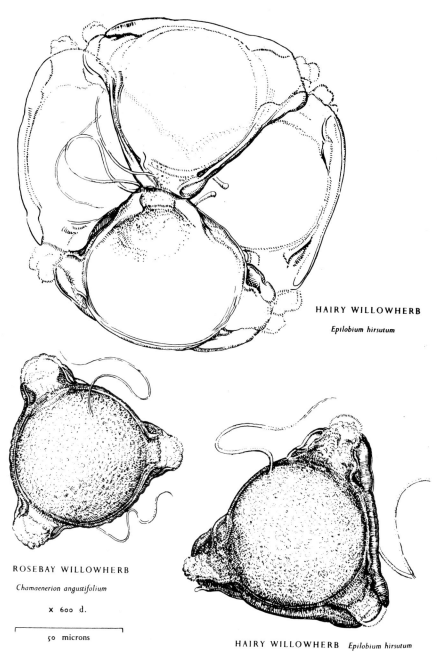

HAIRY WILLOWHERB

Epilobium hirsutum

ROSEBAY WILLOWHERB

Chamaenerion angustifolium

x 600 d.

50 microns

HAIRY WILLOWHERB *Epilobium hirsutum*

ONAGRACEAE

26

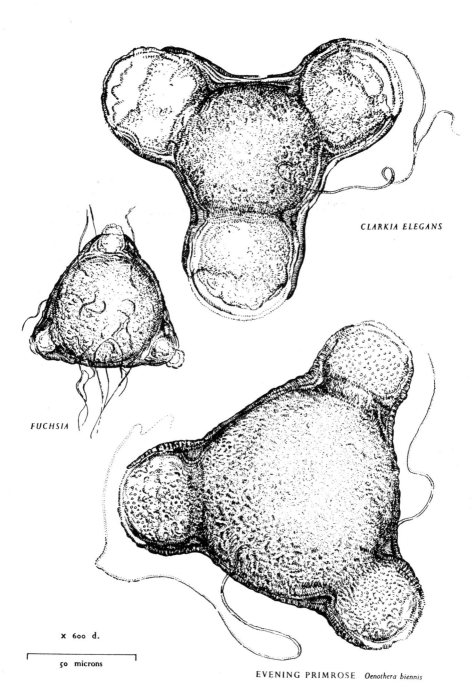

CLARKIA ELEGANS

FUCHSIA

x 600 d.

50 microns

EVENING PRIMROSE *Oenothera biennis*

ONAGRACEAE

27

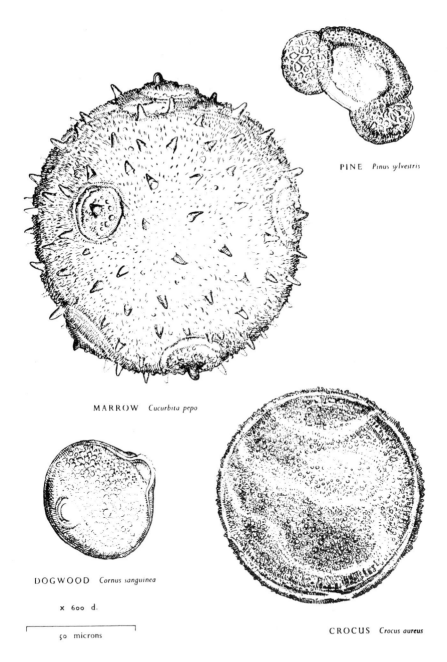

PINE   *Pinus sylvestris*

MARROW   *Cucurbita pepo*

DOGWOOD   *Cornus sanguinea*

x 600 d.

50 microns

CROCUS   *Crocus aureus*

CORNACEAE
IRIDACEAE PINACEAE CUCURBITACEAE

28

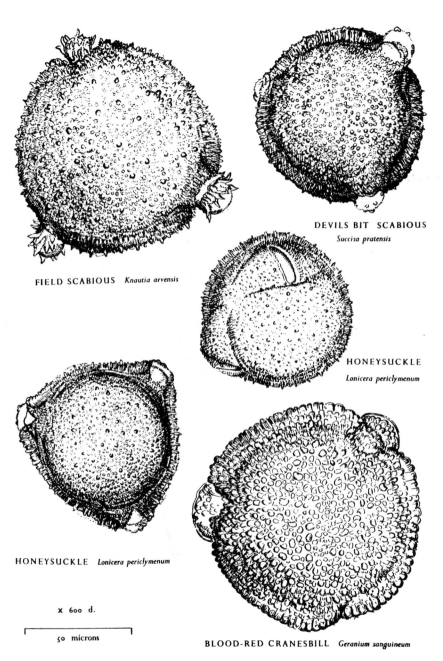

DEVILS BIT SCABIOUS
Succisa pratensis

FIELD SCABIOUS *Knautia arvensis*

HONEYSUCKLE
Lonicera periclymenum

HONEYSUCKLE *Lonicera periclymenum*

x 600 d.

50 microns

BLOOD-RED CRANESBILL *Geranium sanguineum*

DIPSACACEAE GERANIACEAE CAPRIFOLIACEAE

29

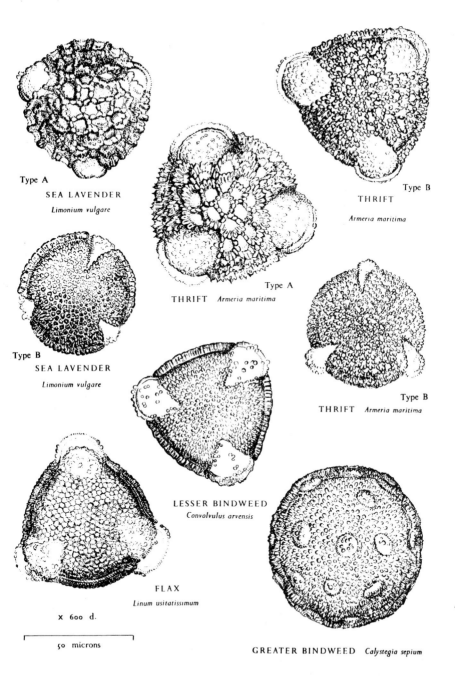

Type A

SEA LAVENDER

Limonium vulgare

Type B

THRIFT

Armeria maritima

Type A

THRIFT *Armeria maritima*

Type B

SEA LAVENDER

Limonium vulgare

Type B

THRIFT *Armeria maritima*

LESSER BINDWEED

Convolvulus arvensis

FLAX

Linum usitatissimum

x 600 d.

50 microns

GREATER BINDWEED *Calystegia sepium*

PLUMBAGINACEAE LINACEAE CONVOLVULACEAE

REFERENCES

Publications marked * are in the Bee Research Association Library

* 1 ALLEN, M. Y. (1937) European bee plants. *Alexandria : Bee Kingdom League*
* 2 ARMBRUSTER, L. & OENIKE, G. (1929) Die Pollenformen als Mittel zur Honigherkunftsbestimmung. *Neumünster : Wachholtz*
* 3 ARMBRUSTER, L. & JACOBS, J. (1934-5) Pollenformen und Honigherkunft-Bestimmung. *Berlin : Archiv für Bienenkunde*
* 4 BAKER, H. G. (1948) Dimorphism and monomorphism in the Plumbaginaceae. *Ann. Bot.* 12 : 47
* 5 BEECKEN, W. (1934) Uber die Putz- und Sauberungshandlungen der Honigbiene. *Arch. Bienenk.* 15 : 213
* 6 BELING, I. (1931) Beobachtungen über das Pollensammeln der Honigbiene. *Arch. Bienenk.* 12 : 352
   7 BENTHAM, G. & HOOKER, J. D. (1945) The British flora. *Ashford : L. Reeve & Co.*
* 8 BETTS, A. D. (1935) The constancy of the pollen-collecting bee. *Bee World* 16 : 111
* 9 BEUTLER, R. (1930) Biologisch-chemische Untersuchungen am Nektar von Immenblumen. *Z. vergl. Physiol.* 12 : 72
*10 —— (1951) Time and distance in the life of the foraging bee. *Bee World* 32 : 25
*11 BEUTLER, R. & OPFINGER, E. (1951) Pollenernährung und Nosemabefall der Honigbiene. *Z. vergl. Physiol.* 32 : 383
*12 BUTLER, C. G. (1949) The honeybee. An introduction to her sense physiology and behaviour. *Oxford : Clarendon Press*
*13 CASTEEL, D. B. (1912) The behavior of the honey bee in pollen collecting. *U.S.Bur. Ent. Bull No.* 121
  14 CLAPHAM, A. R. (1946) Check-list of British vascular plants. *J. Ecol.* 33(2)
*15 DADE, H. A. (1949) Colour terminology in biology. *London : Commonwealth Mycological Institute, Kew*
  16 DENGG, O. (1922) Vollständiger Blütenkalender und Trachtweise. *Innsbruck*
*17 ECKERT, J. E. (1933) Buckeye poisoning of the honeybee. *J. econ. Ent.* 26 : 181
*18 ERDTMAN, G. (1943) An introduction to pollen analysis. *Waltham, Mass : Chronica Botanica*
  19 FAEGRI, K. & IVERSEN, J. (1950) Textbook of modern pollen analysis. *Copenhagen : Munksgaard*
*20 FRISCH, K. VON (1947) The dances of the honeybee. *Bull. anim. Behav.* 1 : 1
*21 —— (1952) Orienting ability and communication among bees. *Bee World* 33 : 19, 35
  22 GORDON, J. (1934) A stepladder to painting. *London : Faber & Faber*
*23 HARRIS, W. F. & FILMER, D. W. (1948) Pollen in honey and bee loads. *N.Z.J. Sci. Tech. A* 30 : 178
*24 HARWOOD, A. F. (ED.) (1947) British bee Plants. *Foxton : Apis Club*
*25 HAYES, G. (1925) Nectar producing plants and their pollen. *London: British Bee Journal*

REFERENCES

*26   HODGES, D. (1949) Preliminary report on the colours of pollen loads. *Bee World* 30 : 13

*27   HOWES, F. N. (1945) Plants and beekeeping. *London : Faber & Faber*

*28   JAXTHEIMER, R. (1949) Die Ausnutzung der heimischen Flora durch die Bienen. *Arch. Bienenk.* 26 : 17

*29   JEFFREE, E. P. (1951) Modified phenological approach in the determination of flowering times of beekeeping (and other) plants in Aberdeenshire. *14th Internat. Beekeeping Congr.* Paper 16

30   MAERZ, A. & PAUL, M. R. (1930) A dictionary of color. *New York : McGraw Hill*

*31   MANLEY, R. O. B. (1946) Honey farming. *London : Faber & Faber*

*32   —— (1948) Beekeeping in Britain. *London : Faber & Faber*

*33   MAURIZIO, A. (1940) Schweizerische Honigtypen 3. Vergissmeinnichthonig. *Schweiz. Bienenztg.* 63 : 47

*34   —— (1941) Schweizerische Honigtypen 4. Honig der Edelkastanie. *Schweiz. Bienenztg.* 64 : 409

*35   —— (1942) Bienen mit Pollenfleck auf dem Thorax. Pollenanalytische Beobachtungen 10. *Schweiz. Bienenztg.* 65 : 524

*36   —— (1945) Trachtkrankheiten der Bienen 1. Vergiftungen bei einseitiger Tracht von Rosskastanien. *Beih. Schweiz. Bienenztg.* 1(8) : 338

*37   —— (1949) Pollenanalytische Untersuchungen an Honig und Pollenhöschen. *Beih. Schweiz. Bienenztg.* 2(18) : 320

*38   —— (1950) The influence of pollen feeding and brood rearing on the length of life and physiological condition of the honeybee. *Bee World* 31 : 9

*39   —— (1951) Pollen analysis of honey. *Bee World* 32 : 1

*40   Mikkelsen, V. M. (1948) Et forsog til identificering af cruciferpollen i honning. *Tss. Planteavl* 51 : 528

41   OSTWALD, W. (1933) Colour science, Part 2 (trans. J. Scott Taylor). *London : Winsor & Newton*

*42   PARKER, R. L. (1922) Some pollens gathered by bees. *Rep. Iowa State Apiarist :* 68

*43   —— (1926) The collection and utilization of pollen by the honeybee. *Mem. Cornell Univ. agric. exp. Sta.* No. 98

*44   PERCIVAL, M. (1947) Pollen collection by *Apis mellifera New Phytol.* 46 : 142

*45   —— (1950) Pollen presentation and pollen collection. *New Phytol.* 49 : 40

*46   REITER, R. (1947) The coloration of anther and corbicular pollen. *Ohio J. Sci.* 47 : 137

*47   RIBBANDS, C. R. (1949) The foraging methods of individual honeybees. *J. anim. Ecol.* 18 : 47

*48   —— (1950) Changes in the behaviour of honeybees following their recovery from anæsthesia. *J. exp. Biol.* 27 : 302.

49   SCHOCH-BODMER, H. (1927) Beiträge zum Heterostylie-Problem bei *Lythrum salicaria* L. *Flora* 22 : 307

50   —— (1940) The influence of nutrition upon pollen grain size in *Lythrum salicaria. J. Genet.* XL 3, 393

*51   SLADEN, F. W. L. (1911) How pollen is collected by the social bees and the part played in the process by the auricle. *Brit. Bee J.* 39 : 491, 506

*52   SNODGRASS, R. E. (1949) The anatomy of the honeybee. *In* The hive and the honeybee, 1949 ed. *Hamilton, Ill. : Dadant & Sons*

REFERENCES

*53   SYNGE, A. D. (1947) Pollen collection by honeybees. *J. anim. Ecol.* 16 : 122

54   TODD, F. E. & BISHOP, R. K. (1940) Trapping honeybee—gathered pollen and factors affecting yields. *J. econ. Ent.* 33 : 866

*55   TODD, F. E. & BRETHERICK, O. (1942) The composition of pollens. *J. econ. Ent.* 35 : 312

56   TURRILL, W. B. (1948) British plant life. *London: Collins*

*57   WEDMORE, E. B. (1932) A manual of beekeeping. *London: Arnold*

58   WODEHOUSE, R. P. (1935) Pollen grains. *New York & London: McGraw Hill*

*59   WYKES, G. R. (1952) An investigation of the sugars present in the nectar of flowers of various species. *New Phytol.* 51

*60   ZANDER, E. (1935) Beiträge zur Herkunftsbestimmung bei Honig. I. *Berlin: Reichsfachgruppe Imker E.V.*

*61   —— (1937) II. *Leipzig: Liedloff, Loth & Michaelis*

*62   —— (1941) III. *Leipzig: Liedloff, Loth & Michaelis*

*63   —— (1949) IV. *München: Ehrenwirth*

*64   —— (1951) V. *Leipzig: Liedloff, Loth & Michaelis*

The author is indebted to the publishers named below for permission to quote extracts from the following works:—

22   Messrs. Faber & Faber

41   Messrs Winsor & Newton

58   The McGraw-Hill Book Company

INDEX OF PLANTS

The numbers in heavy type refer to the Colour Chart

The numbers in ordinary type refer to the Plates of Pollen Grain Drawings

INDEX OF PLANTS

INDEX OF PLANTS

1 LAURUSTINUS
Viburnum tinus

2 WINTER HEATH
Erica carnea

NO OTHER RECORD

3 SNOWDROP
Galanthus nivalis

4 ALDER
Alnus glutinosa

5 HAZEL
Corylus avellana

6 YELLOW CROCUS
Crocus aureus

7 BLUE CROCUS
Crocus sp.

8 ELM
Ulmus procera

9 EARLY POPLAR
Populus sp.

10 GORSE
Ulex europaeus

11 YEW
Taxus baccata

12 WILLOW
Salix caprea

13 SIBERIAN SQUILL
Scilla siberica

14 COLTSFOOT
Tussilago farfara

15 BLACKTHORN
Prunus spinosa

16 ORNAMENTAL PRUNUS
Prunus cerasifera

17 ALMOND
Prunus amygdalus

18 POPLAR
Populus sp.

19 LESSER CELANDINE
Ranunculus ficaria

20 WOOD ANEMONE
Anemone nemorosa

EARLY SPRING

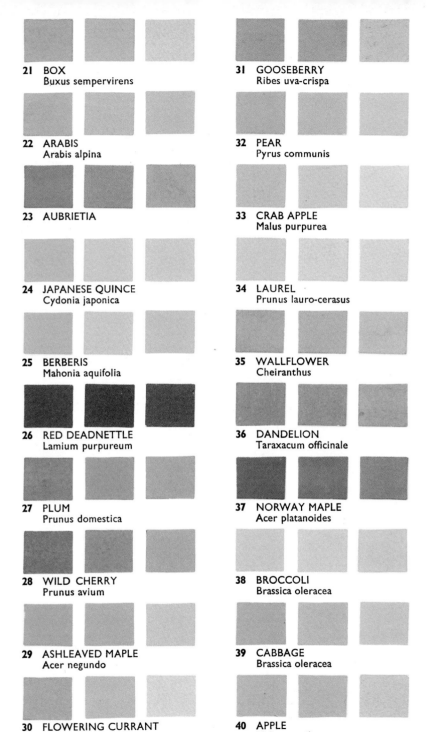

21 BOX
Buxus sempervirens

31 GOOSEBERRY
Ribes uva-crispa

22 ARABIS
Arabis alpina

32 PEAR
Pyrus communis

23 AUBRIETIA

33 CRAB APPLE
Malus purpurea

24 JAPANESE QUINCE
Cydonia japonica

34 LAUREL
Prunus lauro-cerasus

25 BERBERIS
Mahonia aquifolia

35 WALLFLOWER
Cheiranthus

26 RED DEADNETTLE
Lamium purpureum

36 DANDELION
Taraxacum officinale

27 PLUM
Prunus domestica

37 NORWAY MAPLE
Acer platanoides

28 WILD CHERRY
Prunus avium

38 BROCCOLI
Brassica oleracea

29 ASHLEAVED MAPLE
Acer negundo

39 CABBAGE
Brassica oleracea

30 FLOWERING CURRANT
Ribes sanguineum

40 APPLE
Malus pumila

EARLY TO LATE SPRING

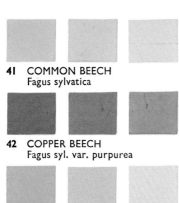

41 COMMON BEECH
Fagus sylvatica

51 OAK
Quercus robur

42 COPPER BEECH
Fagus syl. var. purpurea

52 LILAC
Syringa vulgaris

43 BLUEBELL
Scilla nonscripta

NO OTHER
RECORD

53 PLANTAIN
Plantago

44 GARDEN BLUEBELL
Scilla sp.

54 HOLLY
Ilex aquifolium

NO OTHER RECORD

45 BIRCH
Betula pendula

55 MOUNTAIN ASH
Sorbus aucuparia

46 SYCAMORE
Acer pseudo-platanus

56 WHITE BRYONY
Bryonia dioica

47 WHITE HORSE CHESTNUT
Aesculus hippocastanum

57 BROOM
Sarothamnus scoparius

48 RED HORSE CHESTNUT
Aesculus carnea

58 DOG ROSE
Rosa canina

49 HAWTHORN
Crataegus monogyna

59 ELDER
Sambucus nigra

50 BUTTERCUP
Ranunculus bulbosus

60 ROCKROSE
Helianthemum sp.

LATE SPRING TO EARLY SUMMER

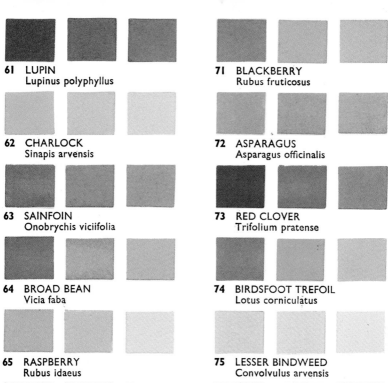

| 61 | LUPIN | 71 | BLACKBERRY |
| | Lupinus polyphyllus | | Rubus fruticosus |

| 62 | CHARLOCK | 72 | ASPARAGUS |
| | Sinapis arvensis | | Asparagus officinalis |

| 63 | SAINFOIN | 73 | RED CLOVER |
| | Onobrychis viciifolia | | Trifolium pratense |

| 64 | BROAD BEAN | 74 | BIRDSFOOT TREFOIL |
| | Vicia faba | | Lotus corniculatus |

| 65 | RASPBERRY | 75 | LESSER BINDWEED |
| | Rubus idaeus | | Convolvulus arvensis |

| 66 | FALSE ACACIA | 76 | FIELD POPPY |
| | Robinia pseudo-acacia | | Papaver rhoeas |

| 67 | ORIENTAL POPPY | 77 | VIPERS BUGLOSS |
| | Papaver orientale | | Echium vulgare |

68 YELLOW MELILOT
Melilotus officinalis

78 VERONICA
Veronica spicata

NO OTHER
RECORD

69 BLOODRED CRANESBILL
Geranium sanguineum

NO OTHER RECORD

79 DOGWOOD
Cornus sanguinea

NO OTHER
RECORD

70 WHITE CLOVER
Trifolium repens

80 PEACHLEAVED CAMPANULA
Campanula persicifolia

EARLY SUMMER TO SUMMER

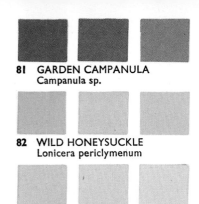

81 GARDEN CAMPANULA
Campanula sp.

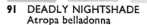

91 DEADLY NIGHTSHADE
Atropa belladonna

82 WILD HONEYSUCKLE
Lonicera periclymenum

92 KNAPWEED
Centaurea nigra

83 CORNFLOWER
Centaurea cyanus

93 HOGWEED
Heracleum sphondylium

84 ROSEBAY WILLOWHERB
Chamaenerion angustifolium

94 BORAGE
Borago officinalis

85 HAIRY WILLOWHERB
Epilobium hirsutum

95 CLARKIA ELEGANS

NO OTHER
RECORD

86 BELL HEATH
Erica cinerea

96 MIGNONETTE
Reseda odorata

87 PRIVET
Ligustrum vulgare

97 QUEEN ANNE'S THIMBLE
Gilia capitata

88 COMMON LIME
Tilia vulgaris

98 CALIFORNIAN POPPY
Eschscholtzia

89 PHACELIA TENACETIFOLIA

99 WHITE MELILOT
Melilotus alba

90 PHACELIA CAMPANULARIA

100 LEEK
Allium porrum

SUMMER

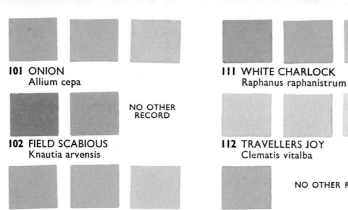

101 ONION
Allium cepa

111 WHITE CHARLOCK
Raphanus raphanistrum

NO OTHER
RECORD

102 FIELD SCABIOUS
Knautia arvensis

112 TRAVELLERS JOY
Clematis vitalba

NO OTHER RECORD

103 MEADOWSWEET
Filipendula ulmaria

113 TOADFLAX
Linaria vulgaris

104 SWEET CHESTNUT
Castanea sativa

114 CHICORY
Cichorium intybus

NO OTHER
RECORD

105 BUCKWHEAT
Fagopyrum esculentum

115 LING HEATHER
Calluna vulgaris

106 MULLEIN
Verbascum thapsus

116 PURPLE LOOSESTRIFE
Lythrum salicaria

NO OTHER RECORD

107 FIGWORT
Scrophularia aquatica

117 DAHLIA COLTNESS GEM

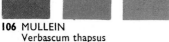

108 FIELD THISTLE
Cirsium arvense

118 VIRGINIA CREEPER
Parthenocissus tricuspidata

109 EVENING PRIMROSE
Oenothera biennis

119 TOBACCO
Tabacum nicotiana

110 MARJORAM
Origanum vulgare

120 IVY
Hedera helix

SUMMER TO LATE SUMMER